Public Assistance of the Poor in France

From the Middle Ages to the Late 19th Century
(New Edition)

Emily Greene Balch

VERNON PRESS

First published in 1893, Publications of the American Economic Association.

www.vernonpress.com

In the Americas:
Vernon Press
1000 N West Street,
Suite 1200, Wilmington,
Delaware 19801
United States

In the rest of the world
Vernon Press
C/Sancti Espiritu 17,
Malaga, 29006
Spain

ISBN: 978-1-62273-041-4

PREFACE

It is obvious that so large a subject as public assistance in France could not be dealt with critically, much less exhaustively, in an essay of this length. Poor law legislation and administration raise so many questions, political, economic and social, and have such far-reaching consequences in each of these kinds, that I have attempted little beyond simple exposition, but I have tried to make this complete and accurate. I hardly need, perhaps, to call attention to the fact, obvious enough from my references, that the historical parts of this essay are drawn almost entirely from secondary sources. Especially in some of the pages dealing with pre-revolutionary charity, I have often furnished little more than an abstract of Monnier's history, justifying myself by his generous motto: "*Voluit alios habere parata, unde sumerent qui vellent scribere historiam.*" My other authorities, being less full, only served in many cases to corroborate his account as far as they went. Any discrepancies which I have seemed to detect have been (except in one instance which I have noted) either very slight or possibly reconcilable. Realizing the disadvantages of this kind of writing I have endeavored to keep strictly within the limits it imposes, and to make it possible to control every statement. My work has been done under many drawbacks and with many interruptions, and has more than corresponding defects, but, as far as I can judge, it is not superfluous. At least, I know of no such complete account, in English, of a very interesting matter. When it is completely superseded by something better, I shall be repaid for the time I have spent on it so lavishly in proportion to the result obtained. I wish also to acknowledge publicly the courtesy and generosity of Professor Emile Levasseur, who was good enough to give me some direction in preparing this account of French charity, and whose kindness to me during a stay in Paris was unfailing.

Contents

Part I

Under the Ancien Regime and the Revolution.

The present constitution of public assistance in France can hardly be well understood without some study of its development. Moreover, its history, though somewhat fragmentary, is interesting from its close connection with the political and economic conditions of various epochs and from the suggestiveness of its facts, which often vividly paint the character of an age or throw light upon some of its obscure sides.

Charity in the Middle Ages.

Its Principles. —

The most obvious trait of mediaeval charity is its ecclesiastical character, but to look upon the church as merely stimulating individual acts of piety and compassion would be to misunderstand her position. Charity as an essential Christian virtue was incumbent upon all, but the church and her officers stood as the official guardians and representatives of the poor. The bishops in particular were bound to care for the needy, especially for orphans, captives and strangers[1]. Moreover, in the order that emerged in Gaul after the storm of invasion and settlement had subsided, the bishops, alone of all the former authorities, remained to testify to the Roman ideals of order, and to stand between the lawless and the weak[2]. They were naturally as well as canonically the source of relief. "Let the bishop, in as far as may be possible, give food and clothing to the poor and to those who are unable to labor," is the exhortation of the council of Orleans held during the reign of Clovis[3].

---

[1] Monnier, "Histoire de l'Assistance Publique," pp. 190, 191. In all subsequent references this work is to be understood when the name of the author only is given.

[2] For the position of the bishops in Gaul and instances of their protecting the cities against Merovingian oppression. Cf. Monnier, *loc. cit.* p. 191 sq.

[3] "Episcopus pauperibus, vel infirmis, qui debilitate faciente non possunt suis manibus laborare, victum et vestitum, in quantum possibilitas habuerit, largiatur. *Concil. Aurelianense I*, c. 6, tempore Symmachae Papae et Clodovei regis." (A. D. 507.) Monnier, p. 196, note 1.

Moreover, it was the constant tenet that the goods of the church herself were but held in trust for the poor[4], or at least that the poor had claims upon them. The council held at Rome in 324 specifies that a fourth part of all church revenues shall be consecrated to the poor[5]. Royal capitularies proclaimed: "The church is bound to nourish the poor." ... "The monasteries owe them asylum and maintenance." "The civil authority shall see to it that these duties are fulfilled,"[6] and in that period of close harmony between the church and the king, a royal capitulary hag almost the force of an ecclesiastical decree. The king had also his particular obligations toward the poor. On this point, too, he was in complete agreement with the church. Charlemagne and Louis the Pious both specially declared themselves protectors of widows, orphans and other poor[7]. A church council held at Paris in 829 urges their defense upon the sovereign as one of his chief duties. He must also guard the weak and impotent, encourage the good, restrain the bad, and listen to the complaint of the poor, for "the foundation of a kingdom is equity and in injustice is its ruin."[8] There was thus from the earliest epoch of the French

---

[4] "Possessio Ecclesiae sumptus est egenorum. S. Ambros, Epist. III. contra Symmach." Monnier, p. 167, note 3. In a royal declaration of Louis XIV, dated July 9, 1646, it is affirmed: "The domain of the church is the patrimony of the poor." Granier, "Essai de Bibliographie Charitable," p. 67.

[5] "Ut de reditibus Ecclesiae quatuor partes fiant, quarnm una cedat pontiflci, ad sui sustentationem; altera presbyteris, et diaconis, et omni clero; tertia templorum et ecclesiarum reparationi; quarta pauperibus, et inflrmis, et peregrinis. *Concil. Romanum II*, sub. Silvestro I, anno 324, can. iv." Monnier, p. 190, note 2.

[6] Quoted by Gérando, "De la Bienfaisance Publique," IV, 480. An instance of more special regulation is shown in the following capitulary of Charlemagne quoted by Granier, "Essai de la Bibliographic Charitable," p. 65. These provisions evidently refer to a special season of famine.

"Et unusquisque episcopus aut abbas vel abbatissa, qui hoc facere potest, libram; donet de argento aut valentem in eleemosinam, mediocres, mediam libram, minores vero, solidum, quisque."

"Episcopi, abbates atque abbatissae pauperes famelicos quatuor pro ista striccitate nutrire debent usque tempore messium et qui tantum non possunt juxta quod possibilitas est, aut tres, aut duos, aut unum. Comites fortiores libram unam de argento aut valentem donent in elesmosinam, mediocres mediam libram; vassus domicus de casatis ducentis, mediam libram; de casatis centum, solidos quinque; de casatis quinquaginta aut triginta, unciam unam." (Capit. 779.)

[7] Lallemand, "Histoire des Enfants Abandonnés et Délaissés," pp. 100, 101.

[8] Quoted by Monnier, p. 204.

2

kingdom a certain infusion of the Roman idea of dependence upon the central authorities.

But there was also present with this, from the earliest times, a tendency, traceable to the Teutonic elements in the nation and already visible in various laws of the Franks and Lombards[9], to localize responsibility for the unfortunate members of society, and to require the lord, commune or parish to assume the burden. This principle in dealing with the poor was carried to its farthest extent in the English Poor Law, but it has been too, in the main, the shaping influence in the charitable legislation of France. As early as 570 a council held at Tours had ordained as follows: "Let every city according to its means nourish with becoming aliments the poor and needy of the place, let the local clergy as well as all the citizens feed their own poor, so that the poor may not go wandering through the cities."[10] Charlemagne proclaimed the principle of local and personal responsibility still more clearly in a capi tulary of the year 806. "As to the beggars who pass to and fro through the country, it is our will that every one of our faithful subjects feed his own poor, either from his benefice or from his own estate, and do not allow them to go begging elsewhere. And where such beggars shall be found let them labor with their hands, and let no one presume to give them anything."[11]

The realization of this principle grew more complete with developing feudalism, which implied, as its ideal, a state of perfect immoblisation of society with which a class of homeless or wandering poor was obviously incompatible, a state in which every individual had in his feudal superior a natural protector. With the weakening of the central power all attempt to require the lord to render assistance

---

[9] Gérando, "De la Bienfaisance Publique," IV, 480.

[10] "Ut unaquaeque civitas pauperes et egenos incolas alimenta congruentibus pascat secundum vires, ut tam vicini presbyteri quam cives omnes suum pauperem pascant; quo flet ut ipsi pauperes per alias civitates non vagentur. *Condi. Turonense II*, c. v. tempore Joannis papae III." Monnier, p. 198, note 1. Quoted in a slightly different form by Granier, p. 67.

[11] "De mendicis qui per patrias discurrunt, volumus ut unusquisque fidelium nostrorum suum pauperem de beneficio aut de propria familia nutriat et non permittat aliud ire mendicando. Et ubi tales inventi fuerunt, sibi manibus laborent et nullus eis quidquam tribuere praesumat." "De Mendicis discurrentibus," cap. 5, c. 10, a. 806. Granier, p. 32, note (4).

3

disappeared, and the poor were left to the mercy of their leige, lay or ecclesiastical. Records exist to show that the seigneur did, sometimes at least. feel and generously fulfil his obligations[12]. Especially was the chateau or the monastery the source of medical assistance. Throughout most of the provinces the *seigneur haut justicier* was charged with all foundlings within the limits of his jurisdiction. This obligation was the corollary of certain rights of succession in default of regular heirs. In Dauphine, where the *seigneur* did not enjoy the same rights, the charge fell upon the commune, as it did also in the north of France, and in Flanders. In Brittany it was borne by the parish[13]. Parishes also might be required to provide for their lepers, whose presence at large was a menace to the whole community[14].

Mediaeval Administration of Charity. —

To whomsoever, as a matter of principle, belonged the charge of the poor, the administration of charity was for the most part in the hands of the church. This charity was usually in one of two forms, assistance in more or less heterogeneous asylums, or indiscriminate almsgiving, often at the church or monastery door. The direct distribution of food or money, the simplest and earliest form of charity, continues to be its most important form as long as the impulse to give, roused by the sight of suffering and by reliance on alms as a prime means of salvation, is unchecked by the consideration of ultimate effects, moral and social. The wretched travesties of humanity that still crouch at the doors of Catholic cathedrals, are but remnants of the crowds formerly drawn thither by this pauperizing bounty, which was only checked when growing disorders and bitter experience taught that alms stimulated the piety of the benefactor at too heavy a cost to the victim. At Paris it was an ancient custom for the king to have

---

[12]For some interesting instances cf. Hubert-Valleroux, "Histoire de la Charite avant et depuis 1789 dans les Campagnes de France," pp. 23, 24.

[13]Lallemand, "Histoire des Enfants Abandonnés et Délaissés," pp. 100-115 passim.

[14]Gérando, "De la Bienfaisance Publique," IV, 484.

alms distributed in the hospitals and monasteries during Lent. Saint Louis especially, *"piteux des povres et des souffreteux, et tres-large aumosnier,"* tried to regulate and perpetuate these alms[15]. At Lyons and elsewhere the clergy organized yearly processions of the poor, in which the lame, the halt and the blind, arranged in order according to their infirmities, displayed their misery to the crowd and thus elicited alms[16]. But hospitals, perhaps, even more than direct almsgiving, were the outlet of the charitable zeal of the middle ages. Their establishment began very early. They were, indeed, a legacy of Roman times.

At first they were often no more than a place set apart in a church, under the care of the bishop, for uses of hospitality and for the sick. Gregory of Tours, writing of the fifth century or thereabouts, says there was such a Maison Dieu in every church[17]. Several hospitals are known to have been founded in the sixth century, and the Hotel Dieu of Paris was established in its present position by the bishop, Saint Landry, in 800[18].

Of course these institutions were not merely hospitals in the modern sense. Under the names of *hospice, hôpital, Maison Dieu, Miséricorde, Aumônerie, Charité,* or *Hotel Dieu* they met the needs of all classes. Under Charlemagne and his successors five classes of inmates were recognized and provided for, sometimes separately, sometimes in one establish ment, viz., the able-bodied poor, the sick, orphans. the old, and destitute children[19].

Though the foundation of hospitals began so early, it was especially in the eleventh and twelfth centuries, when the new outburst of life, of which the Crusaders were at once a symptom and a cause, was stirring France, that charitable foundations were most numerous. Stim-

---

[15] Monnier, p. 291.

[16] Ravarin, "L'Assistance Communale en France," p. 22.

[17] Ravarin, "L'Assistance Communale en France," p. 22.

[18] The famous hospital of Lyons was founded by Childebert, and its usefulness was commented on by the Council of Orleans in the sixth century. Those of Rheims and Autun were nearly as early. Gregory of Tours mentions a hospital in Paris annexed to the Church of Saint Julien le Pauvre. Gérando, "De la Bienfaisance Publique," IV, 283.

[19] Gérando, "De la Bienfaisance Publique," IV, 282.

ulated by experience of Oriental provision for the sick, and under the pressure of the new diseases imported from the East, small asylums consisting often of a chapel, a common hall and two or more rooms, to admit of separating the sexes, were spread broadcast through the countryside[20]. Records of their existence gleaned here and there show them to have been surprisingly numerous[21]. These foundations were generally private bequests and were under the care of the church. A chaplain, subject to the requirements of the founder and to the supervision of his bishop, usually had charge both of the care of the inmates and of the religious services on behalf of the benefactor's soul which were often a condition of such foundations. Sometimes a lay control was established by the founder. In one case, for instance, it was stipulated that accounts and a report of the management should be submitted to a body of burgesses elected by the general or parish assembly[22].

The foundation of asylums does not seem to have been in any way restricted by the civic power, and approbation, if asked at all, probably was asked of the pope, not of the king[23]. In the provision for the country the cities were not overlooked. Toulouse alone is said to have had twenty-nine hospitals[24]. Saint Louis was a liberal founder, enlarging the Hotel Dieu of Paris and endowing various other towns[25]. But the wealth of city foundations was especially due to the new municipal energy. As cities gained their freedom they made it a point

---

[20]Hubert-Valleroux, "La Charité avant et depuis 1789 dans les Campagnes de France," pp. 25-34.

[21]The asylums provided for lepers alone are said, on the authority of Matthew Paris, to have numbered 2000 in France, 19,010 in Christendom, in the thirteenth century. Gérando, "De la Bienfaisance Publique." IV, 285. In what is now the department of the Aube there are known to have been sixty-two asylums in the thirteenth century, of which twenty-one were in the country. Of these twenty-one only one remained by the eighteenth century and this is now gone. M. Leon Maitre is convinced that in the county of Nantes each of the one hundred and twenty parishes had at least two of these leproseries.
Hubert-Valleroux. *Ibid.*

[22]Hubert-Valleroux. *Ibid.*

[23]*Ibid.*

[24]Gérando, "De la Bienfaisance Publique," IV, 285.

[25]Pontoise, Verneuil, Compiègne, Vernon, Fontainebleau. He is supposed to have founded the blind asylum of the *Quinze-Vingts*, which still exists in Paris, for fifteen score of Crusaders blinded by the Saracens.

6

of honor to provide abundant asylum for their own members or even sometimes for strangers[26].3 The guilds[27] too, bound by their statutes to mutual assistance, built hospitals for their members or contracted with some already established Hotel Dieu to have them admitted. Coincident with the greatest growth of the hospitals was the rise of the hospitallers and other religious orders which mark the eleventh, twelfth and thirteenth centuries, and which served as a channel for the intense devotion then aroused. The members of these orders, both lay and ecclesiastic, devoted themselves to works of public utility, such as building bridges, dykes and roads, protecting pilgrims, military service in the East, and especially to service in hospitals, of which they instituted large numbers, and of which they were the usual attendants[28].

But the growth, at this time, of hospitals, which are "the creation of three great social forces, the church, the king and the commune,"[29] has a deeper significance than the renascence of religious zeal or the rise of new organizations. Feudalism was disintegrating, and the attachment of the villeins to the soil, and the moral responsibility of the lord for the welfare of his dependents were alike disappearing. With perhaps less misery there were more poor, more individuals stranded and without protectors, clamoring for help. The narrow solidarity of the city corporations left those outside their ranks in a new isolation and helplessness. It was the beginning of the modern constitution of

---

[26] Gérando, "De la Bienfaisance Publique," IV, 286

[27] Monnier, p. 270. Estienne Boileau, provost of Paris, was charged by Saint Louis with the compilation of a *Livre des Mestiers*, about 1260. This he did, constituting the various corporations in regular form and making rules for their industry. Cf. Monnier, p. 257 sq.

[28] One of the earliest orders was that known as the "religious pontiffs" from its bridge building. The order of Saint Lazare, called into France in 1149 by Louis VII, founded hospitals for lepers. The members of the order of the Holy Ghost, founded by Guy or Guide of Montpellier in 1145, bound themselves to poverty, chastity, obedience and hospitality, and to the care of foundlings (*infantium expositorum*). By 1372 they had in France more than 100 establishments under their direction. An order in Navarre is said to have sheltered as many as 20,000 guests, pilgrims and strangers, at once. For these and further facts concerning these orders see Gérando, "De la Bienfaisance Publique," IV, 282 sq.; Monnier, p. 273 sq.; Lallemand, "Histoire des Enfants Abandonnés et Delaissés," p. 120 sq.

[29] Ravarin, "L'Assistance Communale en France," p. 26.

society in which the "social question" is always more or less prominent and never successfully resolved. It must not, however, be supposed that the thirteenth and fourteenth centuries were times of general poverty. The truth seems to be that, previous to the Black Death of 1348 and the disastrous Hundred Years War with England, the population of France outside the cities was as great as at the present day, and the general level of prosperity high[30], with, of course, the suffering in case of famine or of other local accident, to which a community must have been always liable under the insulating conditions of those times.

The natural consequences of a loosening of the social structure—increased mobility of population and the growth of a vagabond class—seem reflected in several of the acts of Saint Louis. "Any idler who, having naught and earning naught, frequents taverns shall be arrested, questioned as to his means of livelihood (*facultés*), and banished from the city if he be taken in a lie or convicted of an evil life,"[31] is one provision. He also endeavored to prevent the necessity of begging by sending officers, known as *commissaires enquesteurs*, into the provinces to make a list for each parish of the poor laborers unable to work on account of age or infirmities, and to procure work for them[32].

It is worthy of notice, too, that Saint Louis was disturbed by that flocking of the poor to the capital which has always been a cause of trouble in the French body politic, and that, after enriching the Hotel Dieu of Paris, he found it necessary to build hospitals in the outlying towns to lessen this tendency[33].

In the fourteenth century, and especially amid the disasters of its latter half, a general decadence seems to have pervaded France. The charitable enthusiasm which had undertaken so much died out. The religious orders began to fail; some turned into purely military or honorary bodies, consuming for their own purposes the funds intended for

---

[30] Cf. Hubert-Valleroux, "La Charité avant et depuis 1789 dans les Campagnes de France," p. 12 sq.

[31] Gérando, "De la Bienfaisance Publique," IV, 483.

[32] Gérando, "De la Bienfaisance Publique," IV, 483.; Monnier, p. 292.

[33] Monnier, p. 291

the needy, others merely faded away. Many of the orders of men were suppressed on account of abuses and scandals[34]. The same degeneration made itself felt in the administration of charitable foundations, which their holders often came to regard as benefices to be used for their personal advantage. In 1311 the Council of Vienne thought it necessary to deprive the clergy of the direction of hospitals, and to enact that it should thereafter be confided to laymen only, "gens de Men, capables et notables," who should take the oaths required of guardians, keep an inventory and render yearly accounts[35]. This is in suggestive contrast with the decree of Gregory forbidding laymen to take charge of charitable institutions[36].

This breaking down of ecclesiastical charity, the dissipation of funds and the utter want of organiza tion in what assistance was offered, helped to swell the numbers of vagabonds and beggars who, amid the wars, famines and miseries of the times, were overrunning France. The first of a long series of measures, meant to repress or prevent beggary, is an ordinance issued by John the Good in 1350 against the beggars of Paris. All idlers and beggars, men or women, are ordered to go to work or leave the city within three days, on pain of imprisonment for the first offense, of the pillory for the second, of branding and banishment for the third. Moreover, curates and other preachers must warn their hearers not to give alms to those "sound of body and limb," who are able to work for their living. The hospitals are warned not to shelter them, and "prelates, barons, knights, burgesses and others are to bid their almoners not to assist them."[37]

---

[34]Gérando, "De la Bienfaisance Publique," IV, 291 sq.

[35]Cf. the abbé de Récalde, "Abrégé historique des hôpitaux." Paris, 1784; quoted by Ravarin, "L'Assistance Communale en France," pp. 23-24.

[36]On the ground that, being liable to be called before a secular court, they might waste in lawsuits the money piously consecrated to the poor. Ravarin, *loc. cit.*, p. 22.

[37]The entire text of the law as quoted by Monnier, p. 302, is as follows: "Pour ce que plusieurs personnes, tant homines que femmes, se tiennent oiseux parmi la ville de Paris, et es autres villes de la provosts et vicomté d'icelle, et ne veulent exposer leurs corps à faire aucunes besongnes, ains truandent les aucuns, et les autres se tiennent en tavernes et en bordeaux, est ordonné que toute maniere de telles gens oiseux, ou joüeurs de dez, ou enchanteurs ès ruës, ou truandans,

But what could any law accomplish in times such as those in which this was issued, following immediately upon the Black Death, and followed within a few years by the king's captivity and the utter confusion of France, with the Jacquerie raging in the provinces, and Paris in insurrection under Etienne Marcel.

Second Period of French Charity: Last Half of the Sixteenth Century.

For nearly two centuries after this enactment of John's, there is no trace of any serious efforts to restore social order or to provide adequate relief for the worthy poor. None were made, indeed, until the reign of Francis I, the latter part of whose reign— or, roughly speaking, the middle of the sixteenth century—may be taken to mark the beginning of a second period of French public charity. Through the first period, which is practically coincident with the middle ages, charity had been distinctly religious in character, simple and volun tary. What coherence it had was due to ideas of Catholic or im-

---

ou mandians, de quelque estat ou condition qu'ils soient, ayans mestier ou non, soient hommes ou femmes, qui soient sains de corps et de membre, s'exposent à faire aucunes besongnes de labeur en quoy ils puissent gaigner leur vie, ou vuident la ville de Paris, et les autres villes de ladite prevosté et vicomté dedans trois jours aprés ce cry. Et si aprés lesdits trois jours ils y sont trouvez oiseux, ou joüeurs au dez, ou mandians, ils seront prins et menez en prison au pain, et ainsi tenuz par l'espace de quatre jours. Et quand ils auront esté delivrez de ladite prison, s'ils sout trouvez oiseux, ou s'ils n'ont biens dont ils puissent avoir leur vie, ou s'ils n'ont aveu de personnes suffisans, sans fraude, à qui ils facent besongne ou qu'ils servent, ils seront *mis au pillory*; et la tiercefois ils seront *signez au front d'un fer chaud, et bannis desdits lieux.*

"2. On pourchassera avec l'evesque, ou official de Paris, et avec les religieux Jacobins, Cordeliers, Augustins, Carmelites, et autres, qu'ils disent aux Freres de leur ordre que, quand ils sermoneront es paroisses et ailleurs, et aussi les curez en leurs propres personnes, ils dient en leurs sermons que ceux qui voudront donner aumosne n'en donnent à nuls gens sains de corps et de membres, n' à gens qui puibsent besongne faire dont ils puissent gaigner leur vie; mais les donnent à gens aveugles, mehaignez, et autres miserables personnes.

"3. Qu'on dise à ceux qui gardent et gouvernent les hospitaux ou maisons-Dieu qu'ils ne hebergent tels truans, ou telles personnes oiseuses, s'ils ne sonl mehaignez, ou malades, ou pauvres passans, une nuict seulement.

"4. Les prelaz, barons, chevaliers, bourgeois, et autres, disent à leurs aumosniers qu'ils ne donnent nulles aumosnes à tels truans, sains de corps et de membres."

perial unity, to the personality, so to speak, of church or king, or, later, to the recognition of reciprocal obligation in feudal or guild relations. The short half century or more, comprised in the second period, shows great differences. The tendencies that seem to belong to the Teutonic element in Europe and that have been most marked where protestantism has prevailed, come to the front. Assistance becomes largely a secular and even a political function. An attempt is made to establish by law a systematic method of dealing with the poor by requiring the local unit, the parish or the commune, to provide for its own poor, and even to levy, if necessary, a special tax for the purpose. This period is also distinguished by the attention bestowed on out-relief. In his attempts at reform Francis I struck at three main points—the repression of beggary, the relief of the poor in their homes, the better management of hospitals. In each of these matters he laid down rules which his successors, for the rest of the century, did little more than reiterate and corroborate. In the first matter his notable work was the institution of public employment for the beggars of the capital, making it possible to enforce penalties for obstinate idleness. They had often before been summoned to go to work[38], but it is in the declaration given at Saint-Germain-en-Laye in 1545, that it is first clearly laid down that *work shall be provided* by the authorities. The provost of merchants and echevins of Paris are to employ the beggars on the most necessary public works and devote "les premiers et plus clairs deniers de la ville" to their wages.

In case the officials are neglectful the king threatens to seize the city

---

[38] By Saint Louis and John in the laws already cited, by a police ordinance of 1413 and by Francis I in an earlier edict, given at Valence in 1536, which, unlike the others, deals apparently not with the beggars of the capital but of Brittany. Monnier, p. 308, quotes the follow article of this edict:

"Est ordonné que ceux qui seront mendicans valides seront contraincts labourer et besongner pour gagner leur vie. Et où l'on trouvera lesdits mendicans estre obstinez, et ne vouloir travailler à gagner leur vie, ils seront punis comme devant, et outre par forban de leurs personnes, a temps ou perpetuité, du pays ou de la juridiction, à l'arbitrage des juges. Et quant aux bonnes villes dudit pays de Bretagne, comme Rennes, Nantes, Vannes et autres semblables, seront gardées les ordonnances faictes à Paris touchant l'aliment des pauvres, d'autant qu' à chacune ville lesdites ordonnances se pourront adapter."

"Edict sur le faict de la justice dans le ducb.6 de Bretagne, et sur l'abreviation des procez, chap. III, art. 3. Valence, 30 août 1536."

revenue— "tous les deniers, tant des octrois que patrimoniaux"—and to establish commissioners to make the payments. The able-bodied beggars, male and female, summoned "à cry public, et son de trompe" must assemble and go to work at the wages that may be awarded them, under pain of the lash if they shall be found begging after the works have been opened[39]. A decree of Parliament of the same reign sends those convicted of mendicancy to work in the sewers chained in couples[40].

To understand how beggary came to be regarded as a crime and punished with such severity, we should see what were many of these "mendians valides" with whom the monarchy waged a fitful and never successful war from the earliest times until the revolution. The nuisance had made itself felt as early as the time of Charlemagne[41], and had grown with the social disintegration that overtook France in the period following the crusades, but it showed no tendency to decrease with returning order, and was still a conspicuous difficulty in the seventeenth and eighteenth centuries. We must not think of professional mendicants as harmless, if troublesome, individuals. They were a dangerous and more or less organized class. Those of Paris formed a regular band, chose a chief, were subject to certain rules among themselves and recognized various special branches of their profession[42]. They infested a certain quarter of the capital, which was known as *la cour des miracles*, because of the wonderful cures that it witnessed every evening when the halt and the blind suddenly recovered from their infirmities[43]. The fear and horror with which these were regarded by the people is testified to by the belief spread abroad in 1388 that the beggars of Paris had poisoned the wells[44]. In the fourteenth century they lived, we are told, like wild beasts, knowing no law, human or divine, save that by which they divided

---

[39]Monnier, p. 311.

[40]Gérando, "De la Bienfaisance Publique," III, 587.

[41]Cf. p. 12.

[42]DuCamp, "Paris, Ses Organes, Ses Fonctions, et Sa Vie," IV, 6.

[43]DuCamp, "Paris, Ses Organes, Ses Fonctions, et Sa Vie," IV, 9.

[44]Dupin, "Histoire de l'Administration des secours publics."

12

their spoils, and it was most unsafe to approach their retreats[45].

Such were the beggars with whom Francis had to deal. But he did more than try to hold the flood in bounds; he endeavored, by attending to those not yet fallen into beggary, to reach the trouble in its source.

In an important ordinance of 1536 he ordered that the infirm poor, having homes or places of shelter, should be supported by the parish. To this end the vicar, curate or warden was to draw up a list of such poor, in order to distribute to them "reasonable alms," either in their homes or in some convenient place. Boxes, which preachers were to recommend in their sermons, were to be set up in the churches to receive the necessary offerings. Moreover, "abbeys, priories, chapters and colleges," were to hand over the alms to which' they were bound by their foundations[46].

Thus was created, or at least planned, a system of parochial out-relief, the funds of which were drawn from voluntary offerings and from old endowment funds transferred, by the royal will, from their original holders to parish agents. For the capital a more definite organization and stricter obligations were found necessary. The plan adopted was probably borrowed from Lille, where the Emperor Charles V, improving on a private organization which he had found already existing, had established a body known as the "general ministers of the poor." These were twelve burgesses of means and standing, cho-

---

[45] *Ibid.*

[46] Ordinance of 1536, Arts. 5 and 6. Quoted by Monnier, p. 307, as follows.

"Ordonnons que les pauvres impuissans qui ont chambre et logement, et lieux de retraite, seront nourris et entretenus par les paroisses, et qu' à ces fins *les rooles en seront faits* par les curez, vicaires on marguilliers, chacun on son eglise et paroisse, pour *leur distribuer en leur maison,* ou en tel autre lieu commode et qui sera par lesdits curez, vicaires ou marguilliers, advised en chaque paroisse, *l'aumosne raisonnable.* A ce seront employés les deniers provenant des questes et aumosnes qui se recueilleront par chacun jour, tant ès eglises que par les maisons desdites paroisses. Ordonnons pour cet effet que, *par chacune paroisse, seront establis boetes et troncs qui, par chacun jour de dimanche, seront recommandés par les curez et vicaires en leurs prosnes, et par les prédicateurs en leurs sermons.* Les abbayes, priorez, chapitres et colleges qui, d'ancienne fondation, sont tenus faire aumosnes publiques, seront aussi tenus de bailler et fournir en deniers à la paroisse où elle est située et assise, la valeur valeur d'icelle aumosne."

Cf. also the edict of Valence of this same year, supra, p. 23, note (1).

sen by the magistrates to collect and distribute all the funds destined to charitable uses[47].

In Paris the way had been prepared by a decision of Parliament in 1505, which deposed the chapter of Notre Dame from their old charge of the Hotel-Dieu, or great city hospital, with all that that implied of control over the charity of the capital, and gave the care of its management to a commission of eight lay directors. Francis I, by letters patent of 1544, transformed this commission into a *bureau général des pauvres* or general poor board, popularly known as the grand bureau[48]. The members of this board were known as surintendents and discharged their onerous functions gratuitously. It consisted of thirteen burgesses, elected by the provost of merchants, and four parliamentary councillors[49]. Later its composition was somewhat different, but it continued to exercise its functions till 1791 when all its members resigned[50].

This board was charged not only with the care of hospitals and of the poor relieved in their homes, but with the levying of a tax for their benefit. This *taxe de l'aumône*, created at the same time as the board, was to be imposed yearly on all property without distinction of person[51]. Hitherto public charity in Paris, as elsewhere, had depended on free contributions, except in so far as the sovereign had endowed it with special privileges which were in reality disguised taxes[52]. The

---

[47] Ravarin, "L'Assistance Communale en France," p. 185.

[48] DuCamp, "Paris, Ses Organes, Ses Fonctions et Sa Vie," IV, 05.

[49] Ravarin, "L'Assistance Communale en France," p. 186.

[50] In its final form the "grand bureau" consisted of six parliamentary councillors, six *avocats*, a councillor at the *cour des comptes*, two canons of Notre-Dame or of the Sainte-Chapelle, three curates, four *procureurs au Chatelet* or police agents and sixteen burgesses appointed by the wardens (*marguilliers*) of their parish. DuCamp, *loc. cit.*, pp. 94, 95.

[51] Ravarin, "L'Assistance Communale en France," p. 186; Monnier, p. 313; DuCamp, "Paris, Ses Organes, Ses Fonction et Sa Vie," IV, pp. 93-94.

[52] At Paris there was the right to take a basket of fish and other goods from the wagons coming in to market, elsewhere exemption was granted from city entrance dues, from the obligation to lodge soldiers, and from chancery costs. From the time of Henry IV the Hotel-Dieu of Paris was allowed to levy a tax on salt on condition of providing for victims of the pest. A common privilege of the hospitals, elsewhere as at Paris, was the valuable monopoly of selling meat during Lent, a custom which lasted till Turgot put an end to it. In 1542 the Parliament of Paris required the managers of the "representations of the mysteries of the Passion" to pay a sum of 1000 livres to the poor, "because the

experiment of a direct special tax which not only infringed the privileges of nobles and clergy but necessitated a scrutiny into private fortunes was at first confined to the capital, and even there could not be carried through out of hand, as the appearance of the successive edicts on the matter shows.

Beside this central municipal board, or *bureau géneral*, which was peculiar to the capital, there were in Paris, as well as in other cities, boards in the different parishes for helping the poor in their homes. In some places they were established as early as the fourteenth century. These *bureaux de charité*, as they were commonly called, differed largely in their composition, rules and aims. Some were distinctly religious and under the lead of the cure. Others were entirely distinct from the religious organization of the parish. At Ussel there was a *syndic des pauvres* distinct from the church as early as the thirteenth century. Their chief agents were commonly a *commissaire* and treasurer. But it was in the seventeenth century, under the influence of the Catholic revival, and of Saint Vincent de Paul in particular, that these societies reached their highest point of development[53].

Francis did not confine his interest to the poor who could be helped in their homes, but entered with determination on the task of reforming the hospitals, a task which he found at last "chose tres-difficile et quasi impossible."[54]

A first edict, issued in 1543 on the complaint of Cardinal de Meudon, grand almoner, dealt only with the hospitals for lepers, the abuses in which were so intolerable that the lepers were leaving their seclusion and going out among the people to beg. Francis planned a thorough reorganization centering in the grand almoner. He was to learn the circumstances of the hospitals and apportion the lepers among

people would be drawn away from divine service, and that would diminish the alms and offerings."

Cf. Ravarin, "L'Assistance Communale en France," p. 25, 213; Monnier, p. 432.

[53]Cf. Ravarin, "L'Assistance Communale en France," p. 186; Gérando, "De la Bienfaisance Publique," IV, 196; Hubert-Valleroux, "La Charité avant et depuis 1789 dans les Campagnes de France," pp. 46 and 47; Granier, "Essai de Bibliographie Charitable," p. 69. Also see below, pp. 39, 44, 60.

[54]Edict of 1546. See p. 32 note.

them. Local judges were to investigate thoroughly the *leproseries* of their neighborhoods and to report within six weeks to the *procureur général* in Parliament. Bailiffs and senechals were to appoint two persons, "bons bourgeois, de probite et fidelite, resseans et solvables," to administer each establishment[55].

A second edict, issued two years later, undertook the reform of all the hospitals of the realm. It begins with complaints of the diversion of charitable funds to private uses, "from which have followed several inconveniences, namely, that the inhabitants of the cities of our realm .... are obliged to rate and tax themselves to feed the impotent poor, who should be nourished and fed by the said hospitals and places of charity (*lieux pitoyables*), according to their means and the intention of their worthy founders." It requires those in charge of hospitals to hand in their titles and accounts within two months; local judges are to make a personal investigation and report. Parliament is to take action on these reports by removing or superseding the administrators, or otherwise, as may seem best. Those who can prove a proper title may receive part of the funds in return for performing the religious services required by the foundation[56]. Clergy and nobility alike

---

[55]Monnier, pp. 322-325.

[56]Edict of January 15, 1545. Quoted by Monnier, pp. 325-327. "Comme nous soyons deuëment advertis que les hospitaux fondez en nostre royaume ayent esté mal administrez par cydevant, et sont encore de pis en pis gouvernez, tant par leurs administrateurs que prélats de nostre royaume, et aultres qui doivent avoirl'oeil sur iceulx; lesquels se sont efforcez et efforcent journellement vouloir appliquer à eulx ou leurs serviteurs le revenu desdicts hospitaux, et en faire leur patrimoine, souz couleur qu'ils pretendent lesdicts hospitaux estre titulez et beneficiez en tiltre, en contrevenarit aux sainctes constitutions canoniques, intention des fondateurs d'iceulx hospitaux, et defraudant les pauvres de nostre royaume de leur deue nourriture et sustentation, et, qui plus est, laissent tomber et ruiner les edifices d'iceulx hospitaux, et ne se soucient que de prendre le revenu d'iceulx, estaindre et abolir le nom d'hospital, pour toujours du revenu disposer à leur plaisir et volonté; dont se sont ensuyvis plusieurs inconveniens, mesmement que les habitans des villes de nostredict royaume, à la grande foule de nostre peuple, sont contraincts de soy eottiser et imposer sur eux les deniers pour la nourriture des pauvres impotens, lesquels doivent estre nourrys et alimentez par lesdicts hospitaux et lieux pitoyables, selon le revenu d'iceulx et intention des gens de bien leurs fondateurs;

"Pour à quoy obvier .... voulons et nous plaist que tous gouverneurs et administrateurs d'hospitaux ou autres lieux pitoyables soyent contraincts par nos prochains juges des lieux mettre les comptes du revenu et administration desdicts hospitaux, à quelque tiltre qu'ils tiennent lesdicts hospitaux, ensemble les lettres et tiltres de fondation, si aucunes en ont, dedans deux mois après la publication des présentes.

bitterly complained of this edict as infringing their privileges, but did not succeed in preventing its registration[57].

The result was a tacit and successful league of those whose interests were attacked. The necessary information could not be obtained and nothing could be accomplished. The king, however, held firm in his intention "de donner un bon et vrai ordre au faict de la nourriture et entretenement des pauvres malades abondans et afnuans en son royaume,"[58] and the next year (February 26, 1546), a new edict was issued[59], ordering local judges to fulfil the former edict under pain

---

"Ausquels respectivement, chacun en son déstroit et jurisdiction, nous mandons et expressement enjoignons qu'incontinent ils ayent a visiter lesdicts hospitaux, s'enquerir du revenu, estat et reparation des lieux, nombre de licts, et des pauvres qu'ils trouveront, et du tont faire bon et entier procezverbal; et iceluy, ensemble les comptes, lettres et tiltres des fondations, ils envoyeront par devers nostre procureur general, en donnant ou faisant donner certaine et briefve assignation aux détenteurs, gouverneurs ou administrateurs desdicts hospitaux, par devant nos amez et feaux les gens tenans nostre parlement, pour respondre aux fins et conclusions que nostredict procureur général voudra prendre contre eux de tout ce que dessus, sans prendre aucun salaire ou profit par lesdicts juges pour leurs vacations ny aultrement. Et neantmoins, à ce que doresnavant lesdicts hospitaux et maladreries soyent mieux conduits, et l'hospitalité mieux gardeé et entretenuë, mandons et expressement enjoignons a nosdicts gens tenans nostredict parlement qu'ils ayent à proceder à correction et reformation des malversations et desordres qu'ils trouveront avoir esté faicts esdictes administrations, par privation et suspension desdicts administrateurs, ou aultrement selon l'exigence des cas.
"Et quant a ceulx qui se diront et pretendront titulaires desdits hospitaux et lieux pitoyables, voulons que, s'il leur appert promptement de leurs tiltres suffisans pour y avoir benefice establi conformement à la constitution canonique ordonnée par le concile de Vienne, qu'ils ayent à leur taxer ledict revenu selon la charge du divin service qu'ils seront tenus de faire ausdicts hospitaux, et que le residu soit entierement bailie et distribué aux pauvres, et entretenement d'iceulx .... A quoy faire et souffrir soyent contraincts toutes personnes, de quelque estat, qualite ou condition qu'ils soyent, etc."
[57] It was, however, conceded that the lord, lay or ecclesiastical, might, in case of an establishment on his own estate, send one or two good and notable men to accompany the judges in their inspection, "sans toutefois contredire ny empescher que l'intention et bon vouloir fussent executez."
[58] Monnier, p. 328.
[59] Monnier, p. 328.
Rochefort, February 26, 1546.
"... Pour ce est il que nous, desirans de tout nostre coeur, pour le deu et acquit de nostre conscience, l' entiere et parfaite execution de nostredict edict de poinct en poinct, selon sa forme et teneur, comme chose trés saincte et agreable à Dieu le Createur, et les deniersdes pauvresleurestredelivrez et distribuez selon la vraye intention des fondateurs, *chose tres-difficile et quasi impossible d' executer*, attendu que les dicts soy disanstitulaires et administrateurs des dicts hospitaux, au moyen qu' ils jouyssent du revenu, sont saisis des lettres, tiltres, enseignemens et fondations d'iceulx, et different de les exhiber, et par ce moyen empeschent la reformation ordonneé par nostredict edict, et que la valeur du revenu ne soit

of suspension, and, moreover, to seize the revenues of the hospitals and to appoint commissioners to administer them. In spite of this peremptory order the influence of the persons concerned in the irregularities was sufficient to keep it from being carried out, and even an upper commission of five councilors, which the king had charged with its execution, ceased to act[60].

Henry II, who succeeded his father the following year (1547), did not delay his efforts to carry on the reforms that Francis had begun. An edict dated at Saint-Germain-en-Laye and belonging to the first year of his reign, continued the system of employing the beggars of Paris on public works, and increased the penalty for begging to the galleys for men, scourging and banishment for women. The different parishes of Paris were required to support those of the infirm poor who could be helped in their homes; the hospitals were to receive those who could not[61]. The proceeds of foundations and alms must be given over to

cogneuë, et le mauvais ordre, gouvernement et administration qui y a esté, reparé et reformé;

"A ceste cause, et aultres à ce nous mouvans, avons ordonné et ordonnons par ces presentes, voulons et nous plaist qne tous et chacuns les juges des lieux où sont situez et assis lesdicts hospitaux, incontinent et sans delay, dedans un mois pour prefixions et delays aprés la publication de ces presentes, ayent à eulx transporter, chacun en son ressort et jurisdiction, sur les lieux desdicts hospitaux, hostels-Dieu, aumosneries, et aultres lieux pitoyables, pour executer par eux, chacun en son regard, bien et deuement, le contenu en nostredict edict du quinziesme de Janvier, 1545, de poinct en poinct, selon sa forme et teneur, comme diet est, *sur peine de suspension de leurs estats et offices*, attendu la qualité de la matière; en saisissant neantmoins en oultre par iceulx juges, ou faisant saisir reaument et de faict, le revenu entierement desdicts hospitaux, de quelque qualite qu'ils soyent, sans aucuns en reserver n' excepter;

"En y establissant commissaires gens de bien, resseans et solvables, qui en rendront compte et reliqua quand et à qui il appartiendra: le tout nonobstant oppositions ou appellations quelconques faictes ou à faire, et sans prejudice d'icelles, pour lesquelles ne voulons estre differé. Par lesquels commissaires, qui serontainsi establis, sera regy, gouverné et administré le revenu desdicts lieux, baillé et distribué aux pauvres ce qui leur sera ordonné, et feront faire le service divin accoustumé, le tout jusques à ce qu' aultrement (lesdicts pretendus titulaires administrateurs ouys) en soyt, par nosdicts commissaires deputez sur le faict de ladicte generale reformation, ordonné.

"Ausquels noz commissaires, en tant que besoing est, avons derechief de ceste mature, circonstances et dependences quelconques, attribuee et attribuons par ces presentes plaine et entiere cognoissance, cour et jurisdiction en premiere instance, privativement à tous noz aultres juges, et en dernier ressort à nostredicte cour de parlement de Paris." ....

[60]Monnier, p. 330.

[61]Edict of July 9, 1547. Quoted by Monnier, p. 312. "Ausquelles ceuvres, nous voulons toutes sortes de pauvres valides, habituez et demeurans en nostred-

18

the parishes, and the rich parishes must help the poor if they did not wish to see their boundaries overrun with paupers. As for the "taxe d'aumone" created by Francis, it was confirmed by an edict of 1551[62]. The citizens were invited to subscribe on the parish registers the sum which they were willing to give each week, but in case of refusal an imposition in proportion to the means of the individual was levied. The registers, with the subscriptions and refusals, were laid before Parliament, which could accept or increase at will the sums offered[63].

---

ite ville et fauxbourgs d'icelle, estre receuz et admis, avec inhibitions et defenses à toutes personnes, de quelque qualité et sexe qu'ils soient, de ne plus quester, mandier, ou demander l'aumosne par les ruës, portes d'églises, ny autrement en public, souz peines, quant aux femmes, du fouët et d'estre bannies de nostre prevosté et vicomté de Paris, et, quant aux hommes, d'estre envoyez en galleres pour y tirer par force à la rame. Et lesquels si, après lesdits establissements d'ouvrages, inhibitions et defenses dessusdites, estaient trouvez faisans le contraire, nous voulons estre prins et appprehendez prisonniers par le premier de nos huissiers ou sergens, à la requeste d'un chacun qui le premier les aura trouvez, et, par nostre prevost de Paris la verité sommairement cogneüe, estre punis comme dessus, nonobstant oppositions ou appellations quelconques, pour lesquelles nous ne voulons aucunement estre differé.

"El pour le regard ties pauvres malades, invalides et impuissans, qui n'ont aucun moyen de travailler ne gagner leur vie, et qui n'ont aucunes maisons, chambre ne lieux à eux retirer, nous voulons et ordonnons iceux estre promptement menez et distribuez par les hospitaux, hostels et maisons-Dieu de nostre title, prevosté et vicomté de Paris, pour y estre nourris, secourus et entretenus des deniers et revenus desdits hospitaux et maisons-Dieu, selon le recenu d'iceuz."

[62] Gérando, and Levasseur (in the chapter on Public Assistance of his great work on the "Population of France"), seem to consider this edict as first establishing the tax in Paris. There is a certain discrepancy between the dates given by Gérando, ("De la Bienfaisance Publique," IV, 485), for the successive steps of legislation on this subject and those of Monnier, whom I have followed.

[63] Monnier, p. 314.

Paris, 13 February, 1551.

"Henry, etc Comme, pour donner quelque ordre à un grand et quasi innumerable nombre de pauvres qui resident et affluent en nostre ville et fauxbourgs de Paris, ville capitale de nostre royaume, les empescher d'aller mandier leur vie par les maisons et eglises d'icelle, subvenir à leur nourriture et entretenement, et eviter aux dangers et inconveniens que leur ordinaire frequentation pourrait apporter aux manans et habitans d'icelle nostredite ville, plusieurs bons statuts, edicts et ordonnances ayent sur ce este faictes tant par le feu Roy, nostre très-honoré seigneur et père, que Dieu absolve, que nous et nostre cour de Parlement de Paris, et mesme certains articles concernans le faict de la police des pauvres, pour empescher que ung desordre et confusion ne survinst, et que les autres pauvres des prochaines provinces ne se retirassent en icelle nostredite ville;

"Suivant lesquels nos edicts les presvosts des marchands et eschevins auroient fait dresser oeuvres publiques, et enchaisner deux à deux les valides qui se sont trouvez mandians par les maisons et eglises, pour travailler par chacun jour à ces ceuvres;

"Et au surplus a esté enjoint à tous mandians estrangers eux retirer, sur peine du fouet pour la première fois et des galerès pour la seconde.

"Par le moyen de quoy l'ordre et police a esté gardé jusques à present. Toute-

Similar mixed systems have been tried elsewhere in modern times; in Germany and Switzerland for example, and, in the last century, in the State of Maryland. It is interesting to notice that in this same year of 1551 the English Parliament ordered that collectors of alms should be appointed to receive money at church on Sundays "for the impotent feeble and lame, who are poor in very deed," and that, in case of refusal to contribute, the bishop was to summon the recusant and expostulate with him. If he still refuse, adds a somewhat later act, the bishop shall bind him over to appear before the justices, who, "after charitably and gently persuading him," shall tax him at their discretion[64]. It is curious that the English law shows more hesitation than the French to give the character of an obligatory tax to these contributions. In the matter of the administration of hospitals also, Henry strove to strengthen his father's work, "se voulant ayder à ses predecesseurs en ce vertuex desir et intention qu'ils ont envers

---

fois les questes et aumosnes que Ton voulait recouvrer par sepmaine en chacune paroisse sont tant diminuées, et est la charité de la pluspart des plus aisez manans et habitans de nostredite ville tant refroidie, qu'il est malaisé et impossible de plus continuer l'aumosne desdits pauvres, que Ton a accoustumé de leur distribuer pour chacune sepmaine, chose qui nous vient à très-grand regret et deplaisir.

"Pourquoy nous, desirans à ce pourvoir, et nous employer à oeuvres vertueuses et pitoyables, à ce que les pauvres des prochaines provinces ne se viennent retirer en nostredite ville, *qui pourroient apporter grands inconveniens et dangers de pesie aux manans et habitans d'icelle*, et que l'ordre et police des pauvres ne soit rom pu, mais entretenu, et que plus facilement on puisse subvenir a la nourriture des vrais pauvres impotens, avons, par l'advis et deliberation de nostre conseil, ordonné et ordonnons, voulons et nous plaist:

"1. Que par les commis et deputez par nostre cour de parlement, qui ont presté le serment en icelle pour le faict de la police des pauvres, soit faict le plus diligemment que faire se pourra nouvelle inquisition et recherche, *pour savoir, de chacun manant et habitant d'icelle nostredite ville et fauxbourgs, ce que liberalement il voudra donner et aumosner, par chacune sepmaine, pour aider à la nourriture et entretenement des pauvres*, et que de leurs offres, refus et responses, il soit fait role en chacune paroisse; lesquels roles, contenans les offres, refus et responses, soient incontinent portez pardevers nostre cour de parlement, pour iceulx vus eslre procedé, par elle ou ceulx qu'elle commettra en cet endroit, à taxer chacun manant et habitant de nostredite ville de Paris et fauxbourgs d'icelle à une somme de deniers, par chacune sepmaine, eu esgard à leurs offres et facultez, ainsi qu'il appartiendra par raison.

"2. Et voulons que chacun manant et habitant, en quelque qualité qu'il soit, qui sera refusant payer la taxe a laquelle il aura esté cotisé et imposé par nostredite cour, ou ses commis et deputez, soit executé et contraint payer sa taxe pour l'advenir, sans prejudice des restes qu'il pourroit devoir pour le passé.

"Si donnons, etc."

[64] T. W. Fowle, "The Poor Law," p. 57.

20

les pauvres, comme à Roy tres-chrétien, dont il portait le tiltre et le nom il est très-appartenant." But though he appointed a special commission, with orders to devote at least one entire day a week to this business, and though he endeavored to begin the work under his own eyes at Paris, "la première et principale reformation devant commencer par le chef, qui est nostre ville de Paris, avant que de venir aux aultres membres," nevertheless little could be considered accomplished, while the revenues were still in perfectly irresponsible hands[65].

It was the proclamation of the principle of personal responsibility, in an edict issued in 1561, (that is just after the accession of Charles IX), which made an efficient reform possible. This law provided that the holders of the right of presentation, or, where there was no such right, the communes[66] should appoint the directors for hospitals, these directors to be responsible, under penalty of "imprisonment of their persons," for all the property entrusted to them. Accounts and signed inventories were stringently required. Any balance on hand at the close of the term of office was to be spent for some charitable purpose, as, for instance, in helping poor girls to marry or supporting children at a trade. The directors were enjoined to give humane and gracious treatment to the sick, whether of the locality or strangers, and to provide separate rooms, when possible, for incurable or contagious cases. They must not be related to the person appointing, they held office for three years, were not reeligible but were removable for malversation[67].

Five years after this edict, namely, in 1566, appeared the famous edict of Moulins, according to which the principle of responsibility "in their proper and private names for default or negligence" was extended to the officers charged with the execution of the foregoing edicts[68].

But the chief importance of this edict of Moulins, which codifies,

---

[65]Monnier, pp. 330-331.
[66]"Communautez des villes, communes ou bourgades."
[67]Monnier, pp. 331-333.
[68]Monnier, pp. 333-334.

as it were, the preceding legislation, is that it generalizes the *taxe
d' aumône* and institutes the principle of "domicile de secour" or
"settlement," intended to put a stop to vagabondage. Article 73 of
this curious law runs as follows[69]:

"Et outre ordonnons que les pauvres de chacune ville, bourg et village, seront nourris et entretenus par ceulx de la ville, bourg ou village
dont ils seront natifs et habitans, sans qu' ils puissent vaguer et demander l' aumosne ailleurs qu 'au lieu duquel ils sont. Et à ces fins
seront les habitans tenus à contribuer à la nourriture desdicts pauvres selon leurs facultez, à la diligence des maires, eschevins, consuls
et marguilliers des paroisse; lesquels pauvres seront tenus prendre
bulletin et certification des dessusdicts, en cas que, pour guerison de
leurs maladies, ils fussent contraincts venir aux villes ou bourgades
où il y a des Hostels-Dieu et maladreries pour ce destinez."

The enforcement of such a sweeping law as this, was, of course, impossible. As a matter of fact the tax seems to have been established
only in certain cities, and mainly in Northern France. It was perhaps usually employed not as an ordinary source of relief, but as an
expedient for critical times[70].

Henry III made a fresh effort, during the famine of 1586, to ensure
local care of the poor and so to prevent the beggars crowding into the
cities. But it was contrary to the interest of the villagers to retain
their poor, the king was powerless to compel them, and royal edicts
continued to be launched against beggary almost without interrup-
tion. The religious differences of the last half of the sixteenth century were not without their effect upon the development of charitable
administration, and tended to strengthen the movement toward its
secularization. The storm that was to break upon the property of the
church in the revolution seems prefigured in some of the documents of
this time. At the states general held at Orleans in 1560 the nobility
had drawn up a plan "for the regulation of beggary," demanding that

---

[69] As quoted by Monnier.
[70] Cf. Hubert-Valleroux, "La Charité avant et depuis 1789, dans les campagnes de France," p. 20-21. See also below, p. 76, note 1.

there should be levied on the property of the various religious orders a tax sufficient to establish in every city and large borough a hospital for the sick and *ateliers de travail*—that is employment in repairing roads or military strongholds—for the able-bodied. This remarkable plan also called for a *bureau de charité*[71] in each locality, the bureau to be composed of the seigneur, the cure and three notable inhabitants, and to act as intermediary for the gifts of the charitable. It also demanded the suppression of some of the too numerous holidays.

A *cahier* of the clergy, on the other hand, demanded that they should not be called on for more than a proportional share of municipal taxes for the poor, and asked that arbitrary impositions should not be laid on the holders of benefices. It recognized, however, the duty of the clergy to contribute to the support of the local poor, a duty laid down by the Council of Tours in the sixth century[72].

The Huguenots of Rochelle, in a demand drawn up before the opening of the states general of Blois in 1566, went beyond the position of the nobility sixteen years before, and called for the sale of part of the estates of the clergy for the benefit of the poor[73].

The effect of these discussions was felt in the voluminous ordinance which followed the states general of Blois, and which decreed as follows: "henceforth the administration of the revenues of the aforesaid hospitals and lazar-houses can be confided only to simple bourgeois, merchants or laborers, and not to ecclesiastics, noblemen, archers (t. e. police agents) nor public officers, nor to their servants or intermediaries."[74]

This wholesale exclusion aroused the opposition of the clergy, but all that they could obtain was the supervision of such hospitals as

---

[71] Cf. p. 28.

[72] Cf. Dupin, "Histoire del'Administration des Secours Publiques," p. 362.

[73] Monnier, p 337. See also *supra*, p. 12.

[74] Quoted by Monnier, p. 339.

"Et ne pourront desormais estre eatables commissaires au regime et gouvernement des fruicts et revenue desdites maladreries et hospitaux, aultres que simples bourgeois, marchands ou laboureurs, et non personnes ecclesiastiques, gentilshommes, archers, officiers publics, leurs serviteurs, ou personnes par eux interposées." *Ord. de Henri III*, art. 65. Paris, mai 1579; Isambert, "Recueil général des anciennes Lois françaises," t. XIV, p. 399.

they supported themselves[75].

Thus was consummated the movement of which a decision of the church herself in the fourteenth century[76] was the first symptom, and the reforms of Francis I, in the middle of the fifteenth, the true beginning. But the secularization of charity was not mainly important as a means of reforming the abuses which had wasted its resources, but as a sign of the development of the political ideal. Charity had become, in theory at least, a local charge and the subject of a tax, and beggary a contravention of social order. These conceptions had been fully formulated by the close of the sixteenth century, but their realization was far from complete when it was interrupted by the very different tendencies which prevailed during the next two centuries. It would be interesting to speculate as to the social consequences to France had these beginnings been followed up by a period of protestant and democratic development, had they found, say, such a soil as did the laws of Henry VIII and Elizabeth. But such was not the case.

Third Period of French Charity, 1600-1789.

Public Charity under Louis XIII and Louis XIV.—

The seventeenth and eighteenth centuries, or more accurately, the period from the accession of Louis XIII to the revolution, may be considered as the third and last phase of charity under the old regime. The two controlling characteristics of this period are its Catholicism and its powerful centralization. In matters of method the period is marked by an extreme fondness for system and for large and imposing institutions, and by a predilection for compulsory in-door relief on a grand scale. It is also distinguished by the growing scientific and medical enlightenment brought to bear in the service of the unfortunate. Louis XIII (or the regent Marie de Medici in his name), really inau-

---

[75] Monnier, p. 340.
[76] At the Council of Vienne. See p. 20.

24

gurated, in an edict of 1612, the policy more fully developed by Louis XIV. By this law all the poor, not natives or old residents of Paris, were expelled from the capital; the rest were ordered into asylums known as *hopitaux enfermés* or *hopitaux ateliers*. These institutions were a sort of work house, the prototypes of the later *dépots de mendicité*. They were divided into three sections destined respectively for able-bodied men, for women and children, and for the aged and incurable. Cases of acute illness were taken to the Hotel-Dieu. The first and second classes were kept at work, the men grinding wheat in hand-mills, brewing beer, sawing planks and at "other laborious tasks." The women and girls over eight were occupied with spinning, making buttons and with other sorts of work not belonging to an incorporated trade. The food and clothing were to be confined to the strictly necessary. All rose at six in winter and five in summer, and worked until seven in the evening, "or earlier or later if the masters or governors so order." They were bound to furnish the amount of work required, on pain of punishment at the discretion of the same officers[77].

The edict of 1612 was especially aimed at the suppression of the beggars of Paris, and would seem to have met with some success for five or six years[78]. But before the end of the reign the old penalties of the lash, the galleys and banishment were again in requisition[79], and the license and disorders among the beggar tribes were apparently as bad as ever. This state of things grew the more intolerable as the general orderliness of society increased, and Louis XIV, with his love of authority and decorum, felt the disgrace with especial keenness, and did his utmost to end it. "If God give me grace to execute what I have in mind," he writes in his instructions to the Dauphin[80], "I shall endeavor to make the felicity of my reign such that there shall no longer be seen in all the realm,—I will not say rich and t

---

[77]Monnier, pp. 317-320.

[78]See the preamble of an edict of 1656 quoted by Monnier, p. 344.

[79]Granier, "Essai de Bibliographie Charitable." Appendix, "Législation sur la Mendicité," p. 404.

[80]1662. Quoted by Monnier, p. 367.

poor, for industry and intelligence will always leave that distinction among men,—but such that there shall no longer be either indigence or beggary; that there shall be, I mean, no one, however miserable, who is not sure of his means of livelihood either by his work or by regular and well ordered aid."

Louis was not alone in taking the social abuses of the time to heart. In the years 1640 to 1656 a series of meetings was held in Paris by a number of charitable and public-spirited men, magistrates and others, for the purpose of studying and discussing the problem of relief. The outcome was the edict of 1656, the most complete code on the subject up to that time. According to this plan the poor were divided into two classes. The first consisted of *pauvres honteux* and heads of families, who alone were to be helped in their homes. All others were to go into institutions or "general hospitals," which were to be prepared to receive them. To provide for the support of these general hospitals, religious and charitable establishments, corporations and private individuals were called on to contribute; in case of refusal to subscribe voluntarily they were to be taxed "according to the ancient regulations." Parliament, however, raised serious objections to registering the edict in this form, and as finally passed it provided that citizens should be only "invited" to contribute, without being liable to taxation unless in case of necessity[81].

The complement of this system was increased severity against beggary, thus left without excuse. This system was at first applied only to the capital and its success there was apparently complete for a time[82].

Of the two classes distinguished by the edict of 1656, the first had not inconsiderable resources in the private associations, charitable and religious, which, through the example of Saint Vincent de Paul and the patronage of the king, became a sort of fashion and spread widely[83].

---

[81] Gérando, "De la Bienfaisance Publique," IV, 486-488.

[82] For an account of the opening of the Hopital General, see DuCamp, "Paris, Ses Organes, Ses Fonctions, et Sa Vie," IV, 17.

[83] These were known sometimes by the old name of "bureaux de charité," or

But by far the most important part of this work of Louis' was the attempt to provide complete and compulsory asylum for the entire second class. This was to be accomplished, in Paris, by the union under one direction, and under the name of Hopital General, of the principle charitable institutions of the city. The institutions thus united were La Pitié, founded in 1612, the Maison de Scipion, the Salpêtriére, Bicetre and the Savonnerie, making together provision for five or six thousand poor.

A report on the condition of the institution six years after its foundation describes the inmates of each of these houses. One was occupied by young girls and old women, at work spinning. In another were the old men, the incurables, inebriates, cripples, the larger boys, and others kept for one week or two "to be instructed in the principles of the Faith, of which they are absolutely ignorant," and to be then employed, sent away or punished according to the law in case they had gone back to beggary. In another house were children of from seven to fifteen being taught to read and write, or at work, most of them at carpet-making. Fifty-two workmen, appointed by the corporations, taught their trades in the institution[84].

This immense institution, into which it was Louis' policy to absorb other smaller establishments as far as possible, was quite distinct from the municipal assistance of Paris, with the old Hotel-Dieu and its dependencies, under the charge of the Grand Bureau des Pauvres. It was under the charge of a special board and belonged to the "administration de haute police."[85] Begging was forbidden absolutely and under the heaviest penalties. To give alms to a beggar "manually in the streets" or to harbor vagabonds was also forbidden[86]. The Hôpital Général was as much a prison as an asylum,[87] and was so

---

as "assembleés de charité," "confréries des servantes et des gardes des pauvres" and by other titles. They seem to have lost their zeal after a time, and to have shown little activity until the foundation of the Society of Saint Vincent de Paul, by Frédéric Ozanam, in this century. Cf. Granier, "Essai de Bibliographie Charitable," p. 56 sq. See *supra*, p. 28.

[84]Monnier, pp. 344-347.

[85]Granier, "Essai de Bibliographie Charitable," p. 36.

[86]Monnier, p. 348.

[87]This equivocal character of the Hôpital Général was shared by many other

regarded by the people. A special body of police[88], known as archers, or sergeants of the poor, and commanded by a "bailiff of the hospital," was found necessary to take beggars and others by force to the refuge prepared for them. The populace, though summoned to assist the officers, kept all its sympathy for the prisoners and arrests often gave rise to bloodshed. One year, 1658, saw eight armed seditions, and the beggars, turned desperate, banded together and gave themselves up to theft and murder[89]. La Reynie, lieutenent general of police, was obliged to lay siege to the old "cour des miracles," and it was only after his troops had been repulsed three times that he entered in triumph through a breach made by his sappers. He did not, however, arrest the insurgent beggars, but contented himself with razing their retreat to the ground[90].

The support of the Hôpital Général, with its five or six thousand inmates, was a serious difficulty in the way of Louis' plan. Seconded by Colbert he made every effort to stimulate public generosity, both by precept and example[91], but in the absence of a special endowment

---

asylums of the time. La Charité, founded in 1602 by Marie de Medici, was practically a prison. Charenton, nominally a hospital for the sick and insane, had places for the following inmates: sixteen infirmary patients, seven either insane or *en correction*, thirty-five criminal insane, and forty-nine "lettres de cachet." Reports, only too well founded, of the severity of the treatment to be expected in these places, and of the disease which frequently reigned there caused them to be commonly regarded with horror. In time of famine, says Michelet, the poor preferred to starve rather than enter the Hôpital Général. Cf. Granier, "Essai de Bibliographie Charitable," pp. 34, 35, 112, 113.

[88]Necker's remarks on the power of police authorities to arrest and imprison beggars without trial are instructive. I quote from his "Administration des Finances," III, 169.

"Mais en France l'autorité de la police a plus d'étendue; et l'habi tude, la nature du gouvernement, la distance immense qui existe entre le peuple et les autres classes de la société, tout aide a détourner les yeux de la manière leste avec laquelle on peut manier l' autorité envers tous les gens perdus dans la foule, et sans la douceur et l' humanité qui caractérisent le génie Francais et l'esprit du siècle ces observations seraient un sujet continuel de tristesse pour tous ceux qui savent compâtir un joug dont ils sont affranchis."

[89]Monnier, pp. 349-351.

[90]Granier, "Essai de Bibliographic Charitable," p. 34.

[91]Monnier, pp. 367-369.

Louis himself and the queen mother gave 800,000 livres, almost equivalent to the full expenses for one year. Mazarin and others followed with liberal donations. Some temporary privileges were granted, such as a tax on wine entering the gates, a right worth 200,000 livres a year. Boxes in the churches and other public places, and collections from house to house or in church brought

it was a hard task[92], especially in the famine year of 1662 when the Hôpital Général, beside the support of an unusual number of inmates and outrelief to 3000 *pauvres mariés* in the city, was obliged to receive temporarily the country poor who flocked in in such numbers that tents had to be put up in the courts to accommodate them[93].

It was in this year of 1662, when the burden thrown upon the capital by the provinces was most heavily felt, that Louis took the next step and required every important city or town, not already provided, to establish a "hôpital général" like that of Paris[94]. The agents on

---

in something. One curious expedient was an order to priests and notaries to suggest a legacy to the Hôpital Général to all testators and to state in the will that they had done so.

[92] Monnier (p. 353, Note 1), gives some figures for the Hôpital Général of Paris, which may have a certain interest. Unfortunately they are those of the famine year of 1662. Among the chief items of expenditure are the following (in each case I give the nearest round number):

Llyres Bread and flour	350,000
Butchers' meat	115,000
Dress stuffs, leather, sabots, etc	61,000
Wages and salaries (this is composed of several items in Monnier's table)	35,000
Salaries of bailiff of the poor, his brigadiers and archers	21,000
Necessary repairs	14,000
Distributions to poor families in Paris and suburbs	83,030

The receipts in 1657 amounted to 590,000 livres. In 1662 they were 777,000 livres, equal to 2,400,000 francs, or $480,000 modern money, which seems a very small sum for such an institution. Cf. p. 354, *Ibid.*

[93] Cf. Monnier, pp. 354, 349.

[94] Monnier, p. 368 sq., quotes the preamble of this important edict. This document speaks of the Hôpital Général of Paris as successful but overburdened by the number of beggars crowding in, mainly because of "la grande nécessité qui est a la campagne . . . pourquoi les biens de la campagne sont en partie délaissés, n'y ayant pas assez de personnes pour y faire le travail nécessaire"; it speaks of the obligation of each city to support its own poor, and refers to former edicts,

whom the king relied in this work, in which he was keenly interested, were the royal intendents and the bishops[95]. Everywhere he aimed at consolidation and organization. The establishment of small hospitals was discouraged, and those already existing were, wherever possible, united with the hopital general, of which, according to his plan, there was to be one ' in each diocese[96].

In 1698 the organization was pushed a degree further by the institution of common rules of management for the general hospitals. The curé, the maire and the local judge were to be, in each place, *ex officio* members of the boards of direction[97]. The council of state had jurisdiction over all[98].

That such a centralized system had great advantages as regards convenience of direction and oversight, efficiency and economy there can be no doubt. That the great institutions which it created had their darker side is apparent. Though Louis' efforts had at first an appearance of success at Paris, as is shown by contempory evidence[99], they

---

that of Moulins and others; it prescribes a general hospital in every city for poor and infirm beggars, *native of the place or who have dwelt there one year,* for orphans and the children of beggars. The conditions of settlement here set forth, viz.: birth or a year's residence, are those still commonly required in the few cases where the question arises. (Cf. Block, "Dictionnaire de l'Administration Française," third edition, article *Domicile de Secours.*) The poor in the hospitals are to have religious and industrial instruction, and are, under no excuse, to be permitted to stray abroad. As to this edict cf. also Gérando, "De la Bienfaisance Publique," IV, 487.

[95] Granier ("Essai de Bibliographie Charitable," Appendix p. 408), gives a circular letter addressed by Louis to his intendents, urging them to push on the creation of general hospitals and to report to him in regard to the number of poor, the best places for hospitals, the advantages of uniting other smaller hospitals with the new foundations, means of raising money, and finally in regard to the persons who might make good directors.

[96] When the funds of one of the little country maladreries were transferred to a general hospital, the place that thus lost its hospital was given the right to send its sick to that institution. (Ravarin, "L'Assistance Communale en France," p. 27.) Nevertheless, these consolidations were probably a loss to the country, though they may have merely hastened the extinction of the smaller hospitals which were decaying at any rate, and though they must have served to save a remnant at least of their funds to charitable uses. Cf. Hubert-Valleroux, "De la Charitié avant et depuis 1789 dans les Campagne de France," pp.55-56 and *passim.* The policy of suppression and consolidation was not a new thing. Henry IV had charged the grand almoner with the same work and the Chamber of Reformation, created by Louis XIII, had continued it. Hubert-Valleroux, *ibid.*'

[97] Ravarin, "L' Assistance Communale en France," p. 27.

[98] Gérando, "De la Bienfaisance Publique," IV, 489.

[99] Quoted by Gérando, "De la Bienfaisance Publique," IV, 487. See also

were powerless in face of the reverses, financial troubles, famines and exhaustion of the latter part of his reign. The general poverty seems to have been great. Bois-guillebert, in his "Détail de France," first published in 1695, estimated that one-tenth of the population was in a condition of beggary, that one-half the remainder had scarcely the necessaries of life, and that three-quarters of the other half were cramped for means[100]. Vauban, in 1698, believed one-tenth of the population to be given over to literal beggary[101]. La Reynie made a census of the beggars of Paris, quarter by quarter of the city, and set their number at 3,376, women and children included[102]. Beside his general hospitals Louis founded various more special institutions, among them the Hotel des Invalides, for disabled soldiers[103] and, much more important, a foundling asylum for the capital. This foundation was one step in a long series of endeavors to provide for this class, whose peculiar need is so evident and yet so difficult to meet wisely; and it seems well to make a digression in order to treat this subject as a whole, at least up to the revolutionary period.

DuCamp, "Paris, Ses Organes, Ses Fonctions et Sa Vie," IV, pp. 17, 18.

[100]Chevallier, "De l'Assistance dans les Campagnes," chap III.

[101]Ravarin, "L'Assistance Communale en France," p. 187.

[102]Du Camp, "Paris, Ses Organes, Ses Fonctions et Sa Vie," IV, 19.

[103]The question of providing for old or disabled soldiers had arisen long before and had been met as the character of the times allowed. Under Saint Louis and Philip Augustus they were usually placed as lay monks or oblates in monasteries, which sometimes bought off these pensioners—often imposed upon them in return for royal favors—for a fixed yearly allowance. But with time disorders crept in and the places were filled with ecclesiastical protégés. Henry III tried to effect a reform but without much success. Henry IV instituted an asylum in the faubourg of Saint Marcel, and put it in the charge of the constable of France. He afterward added the hospital of Saint Louis, under the care of the Hotel-Dieu. Louis VIII founded an "order in chivalry," under the title of the commandery of Saint Louis, to which all wounded and infirm soldiers were admitted, and which he endowed with the chateau of Bicêtre. This was theirs until Louis XIV transferred it to his Hôpital Général, substituting the present Hotel des Invalides, with its noble dome by Mansard.

Monnier, pp. 374-387.

Deserted Children Previous to the Revolution.—

We have seen that the *seigneur haut justicier* (or, in certain parts of France, the parish, or the *communauté d'habitants*), was required by feudal law to support foundlings within his borders[104]. The cities of Flanders and Northern France especially made early and careful provision for such children. The usual plan was to found or subsidize a Hotel-Dieu, but the method of putting the children at nurse in the country, which modern experience has proved so much superior to the best of institutions, was in use as early as the fourteenth century[105]. As a usual thing a Hotel-Dieu, unless bound by its foundation or a special agreement, refused to receive children of unknown or illegitimate birth[106]. Special asylums were founded, however, commonly under the direction of the order of Saint Esprit de Montpellier, which, by 1372, had charge of one hundred or more such houses in France, of which those of Marseilles (founded in 1188), Besançon and Dijon were among the earliest[107]. Paris was decidedly a laggard in the care of foundlings. A letter by a bishop of the fourteenth century gives a fearful picture of the children deserted and dying in her streets[108]. In 1362 an asylum known as St. Esprit en Grève was founded for

---

[104] *Vide, supra*, p. 13.

[105] Lallemand, "Histoire des Enfants Abandonnés et Délaissés," pp. 105-130, *passim*.
Amiens in 1343 (p. 118), Issoudun, in the same century (p. 122), placed children in the country. Records exist giving the prices paid by Lille for its nurses from 1420 to 1600 (pp. 119-120, note). At Lille also there were special officers known as "gard orphènes," to act as guardians of orphans.

[106] This is true at least of the earlier middle ages. An exception was commonly made in the case of children whose mothers had died in the hospital. Ibid, p. 120-121. At Paris Margaret of Valois, sister of Francis I, founded an asylum known as the Enfants Dieu or Enfants Rouges, from the color of the children's clothes, expressly for children of parents dead at the Hotel-Dieu.

[107] *Ibid*, 124-125. Cf. *supra*, p. 17, note 5.

[108] It is as follows: "Cum igitur, pro ut est nobis a fide dignis personis intimatum, per vicos et plateas urbis Parisiensis innumerabilium pauperum calamitas tantum evaluerit, quod utriusque sexûs parvuli ac juvenes orphani, hospitio carentes, in platea communi nec sub tecto morebantur. . . . Plurimi reperti sunt hi frigore extincti, hi adhuc palpitantes, â mortuis juxta se quaerentes auxilium et non invenientes, simul moriebantur. Multi verò puelli, si mortis tarn horrendae evaserunt gladium, petigine tantum seu scabie capitum putrescentes, ut abominabiles a cunctis hominibus repulsam patiuntur." My reference for this interesting letter is unfortunately missing.

children, but against foundlings its doors were shut[109].

For these poor little creatures the chief, if not the only, provision[110] was that made by the dean and chapter of Notre Dame, in a little house, close by the cathedral, known as *La Couche*. To stimulate contributions for their support one of the babies was laid at service time in a rude cradle by the door, with a sister by his side crying "faites bien à ces pauvres enfants trouvés." In the middle of the sixteenth century a dispute arose as to whether it was by its position as seigneur, or by an ancient foundation, that the chapter of Notre Dame was bound to care for foundlings, and decision was given for the former alternative. Parliament, therefore, in 1552, required the other seigneurs justiciers, of Paris to do their part. In 1570, moreover, it had the asylum inspected and ordered certain repairs[111].

When Saint Vincent de Paul[112] about a century later visited this house, it had fallen into the most frightful state of neglect. The children, picked up half naked and often after long exposure, died in terrible numbers. If they were troublesome the nurses gave them noxious sleeping draughts, or sold them to jugglers, beggars or sorcerers, or for purposes of fraud. The woman in charge confessed that she had never had them baptized.

The saint, grieved to the quick by this shocking state of things, interested some of his "dames de charite" in these babies, and twelve of the little things chosen by lot—since it was not possible to take all at first—were taken away and cared for. Not satisfied with this

---

[109]Letters patent of Charles VII, given in 1445, expressly affirm "que la regie qui d'ancienneté a été gardé de recevoir au dit hospital du Saint-Esperit en Greve enfans approuvds estre nés en loyal mariage et non aultres a ete tout notoire d'ancienneté." Lallemand, "Histoire des Enfants Abandoning et Delaisses," pp. 120-121. The reason given for the exclusion of illegitimate children is that if the hospital received them "pourroit advenir qu'il yen auroit si grande quantité, parce que moult de gens s'abandonneroient et feroient moins de difficulte de eux abandonner a pecher, quand ils verroient que tels enfans seroient nourris d'avantage et qu'ils n'en auroient pas la charge entiere ni sollicitude, que tels hospitaux ne les sauroient, ne pourroient porter ni soutenir." Monnier, p. 392.

[110]I have not been able to ascertain whether or not foundlings were received at La Trinite. See below, p. 54.

[111]Lallemand, *loc. cit.*, pp. 111-112, p. 131 sq.

[112]The following account is drawn from Lallemand, "Histoire des Enfants Abandonnés et Délaissés," p. 135 sq., and from Monnier, (p. 394 sq.), who quotes freely from Collet's "Vie de Saint Vincent de Paul," published in 1748.

partial success, Saint Vincent induced Louis XIII (through Anne of Austria), to furnish 12,000[113] livres of revenue, and undertook the work in good earnest. But there were new difficulties. The expenses grew rapidly till they were more than 40,000 livres a year, and the ladies who had undertaken the work lost courage and resolved to give it up. This was in 1648 after a struggle of ten years. Saint Vincent, however, by an eloquent appeal persuaded them to persevere, and they began their work again with fresh devotion[114].

The king favored the enterprise and gave it the chateau of Bicetre. But the air of the new situation proved too bracing for the children, and they were brought back into the city and distributed between two institutions, one in the faubourg Saint Antoine and the other, near Notre Dame, known under the old name of *Maison de la Couche* or *Maison du Parvis Notre Dame*. In 1670 both these asylums were united with the Hôpital Général, but tbey continued to profit by the devotion of a band of ladies of the highest birth and position who met monthly with the directors[115]. Somewhat later the Saint Esprit and the Enfants Rouges were also added to the central establishment[116]. One asylum, however, was not so merged, namely La Trinite, an old hospital which Parliament had converted in 1545 into an asylum for a certain number of orphans or poor children belonging to families on the regular parish lists. This remained as part of the municipal assistance under the charge (like the Hotel Dieu) of the Grand Bureau

---

[113]Lallemand (*loc. cit.*, p. 135) speaks of 4,000 given by Louis XIII, "quoiqu'il n'eût que la moindre de toutes les justices de la ville."

[114]The words of Saint Vincent de Paul; were as follows: "Or sus, mes dames, la compassion et la charité vous ont fait adopter ces petites créatures pour vos enfans; vous avez été leurs mères selon la grâce, depuis que leurs meres selon la nature les ont abandonnés: voyez maintenant si vous voulez aussi les abandonner. Cessez d'estre leurs mères pour devenir à present leurs juges; leur vie et leur mort sont entre vos mains; jé m'en vais preudre les voix et les suffrages: il est temps de prononcer leur arrêt, et de scavoir si vous ne voulez plus avoir de miséricorde pour eux. Iis vivront, si vous continuez d'en prendre un charitable soin, et, au contraire, ils mourront et periront infailliblement si vous les abandonnez; l'experience ne vous permet pas d'en douter." Collet, "Vie de Saint Vincent de Paul," p. 463, as quoted by Lallemand.

[115]Lallemand, "Histoire des Enfants Abandonnes et Delaisses," pp. 137-139.

[116]Lallemand, *loc. cit.*, p. 145; DuCamp, "Paris, Ses Organes, Ses Fonctions et Ha Vie," IV, 256.

des Pauvres[117].

Now that Paris provided such hospitable reception for waifs and strays there arose a new and serious difficulty. The country around Paris, to a distance of several days' journey, poured in its poor and deserted children upon the capital. In 1670, or thereabouts, when the asylums of the Enfants Trouvés were newly founded, the number of children presented was about 312 yearly; twelve years later it had risen to 890, and by the end of the century it was 1,600. In 1750 it was nearly 4,000, and twenty years later nearly 7,000[118]. More than a third came from the provinces, and of these nine-tenths died on the road or soon after arriving, from the hardships of the journey made without any care or proper food, usually in some public vehicle. To prevent this abuse all carriers were forbidden to bring children into the city, except under certain conditions meant to insure against abandonment, and efforts were made to provide for the destitute children of the provinces in their homes[119]. Nevertheless the trouble continued as has been shown.

With the children in the asylums various methods were tried. The most usual way, both in Paris and in the provinces, seems to have been to send the children as soon as possible to foster mothers in the country, and after keeping them there a few years to bring them

---

[117]Cf. Granier, "Essai de Bibliographie Charitable," p. 112; Monnier, p. 405; DuCamp, "Paris, Ses Organes, Ses Fonctions et Sa Vie," IV, 257; Lallemand, "Histoire des Enfants Abandonnes et Delaisses," p. 130-133, note.

[118]Monnier, p. 400 sq.; Lallemand, "Histoire des Bnfants Abandonnés et Délaissés," pp. 152-153; cf. also Ravarin, "L'Assistance Communale," p. 270, note.

[119]Lallemand, loc. cit., p. 162 and note; Monnier, p. 401. Even in the latter part of the seventeenth century we find the General Hospital complaining that children are sent up to Paris from the most distant provinces, such as Auvergne, Flanders or Alsace, not only by their parents but by seigneurs justiciers and even hospitals. DuCamp, "Paris, Ses Organes, Ses Fonctions et Sa Vie," IV, 266, describes the man who made a business of collecting children whose mothers did not want to keep them, and carrying them to Paris. "They packed them, that is the word, in a padded case strapped on the back; the children were placed upright in this with their heads out so that they could breathe and not stifle in the boxes, which the peasants called, with terrible irony, *purgatories*. Each box held three children. Thus loaded the man set out, no matter what the weather, ... stopping only for his meals, and, at long intervals, to give some milk to the poor creatures. Sometimes, very often indeed, one of the children died on the way; there was no time for trifling formalities, the light corpse was thrown into a ditch and covered with a little earth and the journey continued."

back to the "hospitals[120]." Here, too often, they lived overcrowded, deadened by the most mechanical routine and suffering from diseases due to unsanitary conditions, including want of proper food and exercise[121]. Efforts were made to give a decent education[122], and, if possible, to teach a trade, but the difficulties were many in the face of insufficient means and, in the latter case, of the jealous opposition of the guilds[123]. In most of the Paris asylums knitting was the only occupation provided, even for big boys of sixteen[124]. At La Trinité, however, special efforts were made to train the children in a trade, if possible in one not commonly practised in Paris. In 1671 workshops were established in the asylum for journeymen who would consent to teach their trades, and valuable trade privileges were granted them and their pupils[125]. Finally, however, it was recognized by the directors of the General Hospital of Paris at least, that the policy of recalling children from their foster families to institution life

---

[120]Lallemand, "Histoire des Enfants Abandonnés et Délaissés." pp. 188, 240 and *passim*.

[121]Cf. Lallemand, "Histoire des Enfants Abandonnés et Délaissés." pp. 188, 209, and *passim*. Monnier, "Histoire de l'Assistance Publique," p. 405 sq., gives the regulations drawn up for the conduct of La Trinité, which, in their detail, make a most vivid picture of an asylum for children in the sixteenth century.

[122]Lallemand, "Histoire des Enfants Abandonnés et Délaissés." p. 192 sq. One difficulty was the old custom prevalent in various asylums of sending out children to escort funerals or to beg money directly. Lallemand, 220, 195, 243-244 and *passim*.

[123]The guilds seem to have failed to cooperate with the Hôpital Général where the introduction of trade schools was an integral part of the scheme. The efforts to carry on professional teaching at La Trinité met with not only vexatious obstructions but actual violence. Cf. Monnier, "Histoire de l'Assistance Publique," p. 365 sq., 413 sq.

[124]A director of one of the Paris "hospitals" writes in 1767 in regard to boys placed in apprenticeship from the house of the faubourg Saint Antoine. "Plusieurs de ces enfants garçons, quoique d'un âge raisonnable et paraissant assez robustes pour étre employés aux ouvrages de la campagne, ont été renvoyés par ceux à qui on les avoit confiés, ni trouvant dans les uns ni goût ni amour du travail et dans les autres ni force ni courage; ces défauts peuvent provenir de ce que depuis l'âge de 5 a 6 ans jusqu' à l'âge de 15 à 16 qu'ils sont élevés dans la maison, ils ne sont occupés qu'à tricotter des bas . . . . ; que ce travail pour des garçons parvenus à dix et douze ans, loin de les fortifier et les rendre robustes et courageux, les rend nonchalants et sans ardeur pour le travail; qu'on avoit l'expérience au bureau que plusieurs de ces enfants donnés a des maitres de Paris étoient rendus dans l'intervalle de leur essay et même après leurs engagements, parce qu'il trouvaient les métiers trop rudes, ce qui étoient souvent de leur part un prétexte pour convrir leur indolence et leur paresse." Lallemand, *loc. cit.*, p. 197; see also p. 196.

[125]Lallemand, *loc. cit.*, p. 218 sq.

in the city was a failure[126]. The arrangement decided on in 1761 was to leave them permanently in the country, paying for the girls 40 livres a year until they were sixteen, for the boys 40 until twelve, and 30 until fourteen, when they were supposed to be worth their cost. They were then bound out until they were twenty-five (later the limit was lowered to twenty) after which they were to receive a lump sum down, and, thenceforth, regular wages[127]. As to the success of this plan we have the evidence of the best contemporary authority. La Rochefoucauld-Liancourt, speaking in the name of the committee appointed by the Constituent Assembly to study the question of beggary, reports as follows: "Presque tous ces enfants conservés par les nourrices par dela le premier terme fixé, sont gardés dans leur ma son jusqu' à ce qu' ils se marient, y sont traités comme les propres enfans; le plus grand nombre tourne bien et ils deviennent de bons habitants de campagne[128]."

In all these matters the provinces followed much the same lines as Paris, except that where it was possible they were prone to throw off their burden upon her. In regard to the reception of foundlings there was, as there is now, considerable difference between the easiness of

---

[126]See the words of one of these directors quoted by Lallemand, *loc. cit.*, p. 202. "La plupart des filles restent à la Salpêtrière jusqu' à l'âge de vingt-cinq ans, et alors, se regardant comme libres et affranchies, elles disposent d'elles mêmes; les garçons, parvenus à un age formé, se trouvent sans profession et sans aucune utilité; une partie s'évade, et ceux que le bureau met en métier, se regardant aussi comme libres et affranchis, se répandent dans Paris et dans les provinces; la misère les rend vagabonds et libertins; abandonnés à eux-mêmes, ils si livrent à toutes sortes de vices et souvent leur fin est tragique."

[127]Lallemand, "Histoire des Enfants Abandonnés et Délaissés," p. 189 sq., p. 201 sq. The city of Nancy took this step ten years earlier. *Ibid.*, p. 242.

A commission (of the Paris General Hospital) appointed at this time makes the following remarks, quoted by Lallemand, p. 189. "La commission a observé que ces enfants passant les premières annees de leur enfance dans les campagnes ne connaissent d'autre patrie que les lieux où ils ont été élevés, que c'est les expatrier que de les en retirer à l'âge de cinq à six ans. Que l'expérience prouve que le changement d'air en fait périr un grand nombre; .... que le moyen le plus certain de procurer leur conservation et de les rendre utiles a la patrie, c'est de les laisser dans les lieux où ils sont élevés dés leur naissance et de destiner les garçons, soit au labourage, soit à des métiers, ou à devenir soldats, et d'employer les filles à des ouvrages convenables à leur sexe; que la destination proposée pour les gargons est d'autant plus necessaire que les campagnes sont desertes et la plupart des terres incultes, faute de cultivateurs."

[128]Rapport fait au nom du comité de mendicité par M. de la Roche-foucauld-Liancourt; Paris, 1790; p. 24, quoted by Lallemand, "Histoire des Enfants Abandonnés et Délaissés," p. 192.

the capital and the more economical strictness of the provinces, where it was usual to try to discover the father and make him responsible for his child[129].

In the provinces, too, it is noticeable that the intendents, whom the policy of Louis XIV had made prominent in such matters, were apt to appoint some asylum to receive the foundlings of a district or province at the ultimate cost of seigneurs or taxpayers, and that this arrangement was apparently in process of becoming generally recognized when it was interrupted by the revolution[130].

Public Charity Subsequent to Louis XIV.—

In general the form given to public assistance by Louis XIV was that which it retained until the revolution. New institutions were founded, important improvements made, but there was no change of principle.

Beggary continued to be the subject of much such efforts as had been long spent on it[131]. Nine decrees relative to it mark the reign of Louis XV alone. John Law in 1719, D'Argenson in 1749 and 1750 tried the policy of transporting beggars to the colonies, but without success[132]. Louis XVI tried the plan of having an atelier de travail opened in each province during the dull season[133]. In 1764 special asylums for beggars and vagabonds (*maisons de correction*) were instituted, midway in character between a prison and an asylum and the type of the "dépôts de mendicité" of Napoleon[134]. There were thirty-three of these establishments and 6.000 or 7,000 inmates. Those who had been reduced to beggary by accident or who had a prospect of

---

[129]Lallemand, "Histoire des Enfants Abandonnés et Délaissés," p. 229 sq., p. 235 sq. The *recherche de la paternité* is now forbidden by the Code Civil, 340.

[130]*Ibid.*, p. 230.

[131]Granier, "Essai de Bibliographie Charitable." Appendix, "Législation sur la Mendicité," p. 405 sq.

[132]Gérando, "De la Bienfaisance Publique," III, 588; DuCamp, "Paris, Ses Organes, Ses Fonctions et Sa Vie," IV, 19-21.

[133]Gérando, "De la Bienfaisance Publique," IV, 18. For an interesting account of such ateliers at their best, cf. Hubert-Valleroux, "La Charité avant et depuis 1789 dans les Campagnes de France," pp. 64-71, 87.

[134]Gérando, "De la Bienfaisance Publique," IV, 588.

help at home were not detained, and those who were willing to work received an earlier discharge[135]. Necker was much interested in these institutions, and took especial pains with the institution at Soissons, which he wished to make a model for others.

Nevertheless we find Louis, in 1777, writing to Amelot in great distress over the beggars to be seen in the streets of Paris and Versailles, and beggary was a subject very prominent in men's minds and mouths during all the last quarter of the century[136].

In the matter of out-relief, as well as of beggary, new efforts were made, in general along familiar lines. In 1740[137] Parliament enacted that there must be one *bureau des pauvres* for every parish, unless in cities where the bishop might prefer a union of the various parishes. A tax was to be levied, at the rate of one sou the livre, on the revenue alike of private persons and of religious and secular corporations, charitable asylums alone excepted. This tax was to be paid fortnightly under pain of double payment if delayed. These bureaus were to provide spinning and other work for women and children, "à la charge de rendre sur le provenu de leur travail, le prix des Glasses et autres choses qu' on avait fournies pour cet effet." The bureaus were also to provide bread below cost[138].

But the chief advance made by charity in the eighteenth century, and especially during the reign of Louis XVI, was in the domain of medical assistance. Gratuitous consultations outside the hospital had been begun in the reign of Louis XIV[139]. An innovation of the suc-

---

[135]Dupin, "Histoire de l'Administration des Secours Publics."

[136]Quoted by DuCamp, "Paris, Ses Organes, Ses Fonctions et Sa Vie," IV, 511. Louis' plan is given in a nutshell. "*Aux valides le travail, aux invalides les hôpitaux, et les maisons de force à tous ceux qui rfsistent aux bienfails de la loy.*"

[137]Dupin, "Histoire de l'Administration des Secours Publics."

[138]This latter form of assistance when carried out as a general policy belongs rather to the political or economic history of France. The *greniers d'abondance* of the old regime, the *caisse de boulangerie* of Napoleon III, might be fruitfully studied, but involve too much to be entered into here.

[139]Originated apparently in 1630 by Dr. Théophraste Renaudot, who was, however, forbidden to continue his consultations, as infringing the privileges of the faculty of Medicine. When he appeared to plead his cause he brought a number of his poor clients with him. This inventive spirit was the creator of journalism in France and the editor of the first "gazette" there, and also the

ceeding reign was the sending of chests of assorted drugs into the country to be dispensed to the poor[140]. But most important was the improvement in the internal management and hygiene of the hospitals and in the treatment of special classes of sufferers, which an increased medical knowledge made possible. Public attention was particularly directed to hospital reform after the burning of the Hotel Dieu of Paris in 1772, which drew attention to the horrible condition into which that institution had fallen. The effects of mediaeval ignorance and carelessness had been intensified by the constant overcrowding due to the growth of the city and to the catholic nature of the institution, which received the overflow of all the other hospitals in times of crisis. Louis XVI became personally interested, and a commission including such men as Laplace, Lavoisier, Bailly and Tenon was appointed from the Academie des Sciences to make investigations and to consider reforms[141]. The memoirs of Tenon, published in 1788[142], show the old condition to have been incredibly bad. For 3,418 patients there were only 1,219 beds, and not only did four and six patients share a bed, but patients suffering from every sort of ill,—accidents, madness, fever, small pox,—were laid side by side. The hygiene in other respects was of a piece with this and the mortality what might have been expected[143].

---

author of a much-talked-of employment agency. He also opened a charitable pawnshop which, though closed by Parliament, probably helped to bring about the creation of official *Monts de Piété*. Cf. Granier, "Essai de Bibliographie Charitable" (see Renaudot, in index).

[140]In 1769 Louis XV had 774 chests made up according to the advice of the first royal physician, and sent to hisintendants in the different generalities of the kingdom for use in the treatment of epidemics. In 1776 an annual distribution of 2,258 chests was ordered for gratuitous dispensation to the poor in the country districts. Cf. Monnier, p. 501, note; Hubert-Valleroux, "LaCharité avant et depuis 1789 dans les Campagnes de France," p. 63.

[141]Gérando, "De la Bienfaisance Publique," IV, 303-304.

[142]"Mémoires sur les Hôpitaux de Paris, imprimés par ordre du Roi avec figures en taille-douce." Paris. Pierre, 1788. Of the four memoirs included in this volume, two are devoted to the Hotel Dieu, two to the description of the forty-eight other hospitals or asylums of Paris.

[143]Cf. DuCamp, "Paris, Ses Organes, Ses Fonctions et Sa Vie," IV, 173. Contrast with this a description of the same hospital in the "Cosmographie" of Belleforest, published in 1575. "L'hostel Dieu, une des maisons les plus belles de France et en laquelle la charité est si grande que c'est un vrai sein et retraite de tous misérables; et de telle dévotion que plusieurs grands et riches hommes s'y font porter étant malades pour y trê traités vu le bon ordre qu'on y met,

These revelations, and the resulting discussions in the Academy and elsewhere, brought up the whole question of the utility of hospitals. In the doctrinaire spirit of the times the most absolute theories found their supporters. Some wished to see hospitals abandoned entirely and the sick poor treated only in their homes.[144]Others wished a hospital in every parish. The commission of the Academy recommended a middle course, the establishment of four general and of several special hospitals.

Necker, in his work "De l'Administration des Finances de la France," contributed to this discussion a sensible defense of hospitals from a social point of view[145], but he also did a great deal to raise the standard of existing institutions, especially through the foundation of a model hospital, publishing its accounts in full yearly and otherwise supplying information and experience[146]. Another valuable foundation was the first clinical hospital established by Lamartinière, surgeon to Louis XV.

The crusade of Philippe Pinel[147] against the barbarous treatment of the insane, the invention by Valentine Haüy of the raised type for the blind which has opened to them such new possibilities, the invention by the Abbé l'Epéé of the language of signs, and the system of education of deaf mutes worked out by him with the Abbé Sicard,

---

les soins des religieuses qui y servent et la netteté du lieu." Quoted by Granier, "Essai de Bibliographie Charitable," p. 110.

[144]The author of an "Essai sur L' Etablissement des Hopitaux dans les Grandes Villes," points out with excellent practical sense the inconvenience, not to say the impossibility, of such a course, especially in face of the existence of a class of homeless poor. For this and other discussions of the question see Monnier, p. 448 sq.

[145]This discussion, though a century old, is as much to the point as the articles in the magazines today. The objection commonly brought against hospitals is, Necker says, that they encourage laziness and do away with the need of saving against the time of age and weakness. His conclusion is that if reliance on them sometimes weakens thrift, it preserves, at other times, from despair. See Monnier, p. 451.

[146]The hospital which still bears his name was founded in 1779. It was found that it could care for 1,800 patients a year at a cost of about 17 sols a day for each. It received only the very poor, and these had no need of favor to be admitted. It sufficed in this way for two parishes, or about one-seventh of the population of Paris. Madam Necker herself was devoted to its service.

[147]For some interesting detail in regard to Pinel, see Du Camp, "Paris, Ses Organes, Ses Fonctions, et Sa Vie," IV, 406 sq.

were victories for humanity begun at least during the last years of the old regime.

The reforming ardor which marked the eve of the revolution was, indeed, as conspicuous in social as in political matters. This was the time of the so-called *philanthropes* who, filled with the new humanitarian spirit, represented much of what was best in the ferment of that period. In 1780 was founded the famous *Société Philanthropique*, which, outgrowing a certain vagueness and sentimentality with which perhaps it might here been reproached at its origin, has come to be a wise and successful leader in the private charity of France to-day. But even in its earliest phase it did good and efficient service, especially in reforming the prisons. It had also the honor of being the patron of Haüy, and his institution for the blind, which was the origin of the *Institut National des Jeunes Aveugles*.

But from all such special and partial reforms attention was soon diverted to the radical schemes for providing for the poor that were inaugurated by the revolution, and the old regime, in charity as in other matters, was brought to an abrupt close.

The Revolution and Public Assistance.

The men of the revolution believed that in matters of public assistance, as in everything else, a clean sweep might be made of the past and a complete and philosophical system concocted *de novo*. This attitude gives to much of their work the permanent interest that belongs to the discussion of principles, but what they accomplished was singularly different from what they promised—was, indeed, little but destruction and waste. The committee for the extinction of beggary[148], which suggests by its name the Utopian expectations of the Constituent Assembly which created it, took into consideration the whole question of poverty and relief, and its president, the Duke de La Rochefoucauld-Liancourt, submitted seven very interesting and valu-

---

[148] Monnier, p. 457, gives the list of the members of this committee.

able reports[149], representing in the main the ideals of the *économistes* and *philanthropes*, and embodying the results of many of the discussions of the preceding years. The right of every man to his subsistence was affirmed, but the dangers of an attempt to guarantee employment were ably pointed out and the function of government shown to be the encouragement of national prosperity by general measures. In regard to relief the committee advocated making it a national charge, the funds, at least the major part of them, to be furnished by yearly appropriations as part of the regular budget. They were to be then distributed among the departments on a somewhat complicated basis involving the population, extent of territory, and taxes paid in each district. Moreover, to insure perfect equality, the shares were to be reckoned in units of a day's labor, since the value of money differed considerably in different localities. The department, having received its share, was to distribute it in turn among the smaller local divisions in the same way.

The committee also recommended the sale of the estates of all hospitals and charitable asylums; but as the times were not yet ripe for this wholesale measure they suggested that the revenues of the hospitals, etc., already considerably diminished by the loss of their former privileges, should simply be counted in as part of the shares to be received by the places where they were established. The allowances granted to the departments were to consist of two parts, one of which was to be used to provide employment and was to be paid only on condition of a certain supplementary local appropriation. The entire sum necessary for national assistance, according to this scheme, was estimated at 51,500,000 livres. The old charity, it was caculated, had had only 38,000,000 or so to dispose of, of which 7,500,000 were supplied by the state[150].

---

[149]Cf. Granier, "Essai de Bibliographie Charitable," No. 1342. For a considerable discussion, with generous excerpts, of these reports, see Monnier, pp. 457-478. See also Hubert-Valleroux, "La Charité avant et depuis 1789 dans les Campagnes de France," pp. 78-95; Gérando, "De La Bienfaisance Publique," IV, 490 sq.

[150]Hubert-Valleroux, "La Charité avant et depuis 1789 dans les campagnes de France," p. 89. See below, p. 70.

Such were some of the main features of these reports, the best legacy of the revolution in matters of charity. Their discussion did not fall within the scope of the Constituent Assembly, however,. which contented itself with proclaiming in the "Déclaration des droits de l'homme et du citoyen"[151] of September 3, 1791: "Il sera créé et organise un établissement général de secours publics pour eléver les enfants abandonnés, soulager les pauvres infirmes et fournir du travail aux pauvres valides qui n'auraient pas pu s'en procurer." In the domain of actual legislation it merely voted certain temporary grants to replace the losses involved in its sweeping financial reforms which had seriously crippled many charities[152], and passed certain laws of detail[153].

The Legislative Assembly, like the Constituant, listened to the reports of its committee on relief, known as the *comité de secours publics*[154], and left matters practically in *statu quo*, except for the increased financial embarrassment of existing charities. The schemes put forth bore a general likeness to those of the preceding Assembly, but were more theoretical and extreme. They were marked by the strong prejudice against hospitals and asylums felt by all this school, a prejudice due not only to the former excessive reliance on institutions, to the abuses and scandals connected with them, and to their close connection with the monarchy and the church, but also to an extreme dread of mortmain, of all corporations within the state. But perhaps the chief reproach| against the ancient foundations, especially those devoted to special classes of sufferers, was the *inequality* of the assistance offered and the neglect of I the rural districts. This difficulty, which still exists, is a practical one and hard to resolve, but

---

[151]"Acte Constitutionel", September 3, 1791, "Déclaration des droits de l'homme et du citoyen", Acts XVII, titre premier.

[152]The Comité de la Mendicité reported that hospitals and asylums had lost ten million livres, or more than a third of their revenue, by the suppression of tithes and feudal rights. Hubert-Valleroux, *loc. cit.*, p. 79, p. 93. The obligations of seigneurs toward foundlings was also abolished by the Constituent Assembly. See Lallemand, "Histoire des Enfants Abandonnés et Délaissés," p. 254.

[153]Monnier, p. 479; Gérando, "De la Bienfaisance Publique," p. 491.

[154]For an account of the report of this committee, presented by Bernard d'Airy, see Monnier, pp. 480-488.

the spirit of the times was absolute and preferred no relief to relief unjustly distributed[155].

The Convention, unlike its predecessors, proceeded to convert their propositions into law, but in so impractical and fanatical a spirit that they could never have been carried out. It began by reaffirming in the Constitution of 1793, the favorite tenets of the revolution. "Les secours publics sont une dette sacrée. La Société doit la subsistance aux citoyens malheureux, soit en leur procurant du travail, soit en assurant les moyens d'exister à ceux qui sont hors d'état de travailler." [156]

The first important law was that of March 19, 1793[157], which undertook to establish a complete system of public aid modeled upon the reports of the preceding assemblies. This provided that all charitable foundations as well as the property of asylums should be appropriated and their real estate sold. The whole sum of charitable resources, due partly to this source, partly to an annual appropriation of the legislature, was to be distributed among the departments and finally entrusted to gratuitous cantonal boards for distribution among the registered poor. One-fifth part, however, was to be set aside before the division as a provision against unforeseen needs. Though outrelief and relief by employment were to be the rule, there were obviously cases which these means failed to meet, and hospitals, rehabilitated under the new name of "maisons de santé," were to be established for the homeless and uncared-for sick, and asylums provided for foundlings and the aged or infirm. Another feature of this scheme was a system of gratuitous medical assistance for the rural districts as well as the cities. All giving of alms, after these measures should have been executed, was forbidden, but those who wished to give might contribute to the relief fund of the canton and have their names proclaimed over the *autel de la patrie* on national holidays.

This enactment was followed by some severe legislation[158] against

---

[155]Cf. Ravarin, "L'Assistance Communale en France, pp. 29-31.

[156]Monnier, p. 489.

[157]*Ibid*, p. 489 sq. Gréando, "De la Bienfaisance Publique," p. 492 sq.

[158]Decree of 24 Vendémiaire, An II (October 15,1793). See Monnier, p. 492

beggary, which was supposed to be of only temporary application however, as all necessity for poverty was to disappear. *Dépôts de répression*, or workhouses, were to be kept up, but a mendicant convicted for the third time was to be transported to Madagascar for eight years. By a special law passed in June of this year, a maternity hospital was to be provided in every district, and easy relief given to the mothers of illegitimate children[159].

This plan was full of inconsistencies and oversights, which would have been speedily brought to light if it had ever been put into practice, but they were nothing compared to the fantastic decree of May 11, 1794[160], voted without discussion on the recommendation of Barère as "reporter" of the committee of public safety. This decree is curious as a symptom of the times rather than interesting as a piece of serious legislation. Every decade a "grand livre de la bienfaisance nationale" was to be opened in the temples, on which were to be inscribed the pensioners of the republic. Of these there were several classes, aged or infirm farmers, shepherds or country artisans, mothers with more than two children, and widows or invalid women. The pensions ranged from 120 to 160 francs. The first payments were to be made at the *fête de malheur* with appropriate antique ceremonies. The most curious part of this arrangement was that the law fixed a maximum number of pensioners to be allowed to each department, so that, it would seem, the injustice of the old system would have been insignificant in comparison with what this would have caused[161].

---

sq.

[159]Lallemand, "Histoire des Enfants Abandonnés et Délaissés," p. 257.

[160]Monnier, p. 495 sq.

[161]It is interesting to compare the estimates of La Rochefoucauld-Liancourt and Barère.

La Rochefoucauld sets the expenses thus—

50,000 sick, at 12 to 15 sous a day, or 200 to 250 livres a year	12,000,000
500,000 receiving regular aid, 50 to 60 livres (aged, infirm and children)	27,500,000
Expense of providing employment, 60,000 livres each department	5,000,000
Expenses for repressing beggary (houses of correction, etc.), lately 1,500,000, should not be much more for new measures; with transportation, about	3,000,000
For reserve fund and expenses of administration....	4,000,000
	51,500,000

But this gorgeous scheme existed only on paper, and all that remains of the legislation of the convention is some unimportant regulations in regard to the *domicile de secours*[162]. Practically the only thing accomplished by the ambitious attempt to revolutionize the whole existing organization, was the spoliation of the old foundations and the paralysis of all means of relief at the very moment of greatest need. In 1792 the Sisters of Charity were driven out of France, and two years later the property of asylums and other foundations was confiscated and offered for sale, despite the protest of the districts thus left helpless[163]. To meet the most pressing needs, grants were, from time to time allowed, but currency was depreciated and payments were irregular, and the confusion was complete.

Reorganization.

In spite of the temporary annihilation of charity, the attempt of the revolution to destroy was, in a broad sense, almost as futile as its attempt to create. With the return of order the old institutions largely reappeared like figures on an ill-washed slate. The first to revive were the hospitals and *hospices*. The Convention itself, convinced by the logic of facts, had put an end to the sale of their estates. The Di-

---

Barere's calculation is—

Pensions for 84,000 poor fanners, old or disabled 5,440,000 Pensions for 17,000 poor artisans, old or disabled livin the country 1,734,000 Pensions for 29,750 poor mothers, with at least three children 2,380,000 Pensions for 12,750 poor widows or disabled women. 1,020,000 Out relief in rural communes and in towns of 3000 souls and less. 1,665 health officers, three for each district, one at 500 livres, two others at 350, making for the Republic. 826,000 4,440 boxes of remedies; eight for each district at 30 livreseach 133,200 Provisions of rice and potatoes at 50 livres a district.. 27,750 From calculations made by committee, sick poor estimated at 38 or 39 each district, 21,250 in all. 5,312 children at 6 sous a day, or a year 581,664 15,938 adults or old persons at 10 sous a day, or a year, 2,908,685.

See Monnier, pp. 471-472, 502-503. 15,051,299.

[162] Cf. Ravarin, "L'Assistance Communale en France," pp. 331-332.

[163] For the distress caused by these measures cf. Hubert-Valleroux, "La Charité avant et depuis 1789 dans les Campagnes de France," pp. 51-54, 105, 106, 108. Even Barère was already appalled in 1793 at the increase of beggary, "cette lèpre de la monarchie." Hubert-Valleroux, *loc. cit.*, 108. Cf. too, Monnier, pp. 504-505.

rectory restored to them the possession of those that had not been sold, with promises of compensation for the others[164]. Nevertheless they were so poor that they could not pay the taxes on what they had recovered. Napoleon did his best to set them effectually on their feet again, dividing an annual income of 4,000,000 francs among them in proportion to their losses, and calling back the Sisters of Charity to serve in them. They were still sadly crippled however, while the demands on them were greater than ever. Taine estimates that there were a half or a third as many places and three times as many applicants as before the revolution[165].

The next step, also taken by the Directory[166], was the establishment of communal boards, known as *bureaux de bienfaisance*, to distribute out-relief and to act as representatives of the poor, both in receiving gifts and legacies and in collecting a tax, levied for their benefit by this same law, upon theatres, balls, concerts and other amusements. Both the boards, and the tax were, essentially, old institutions revived. The latter—then, as now, commonly called the *droit des pauvres*—had been established by Louis XIV[167]. The former were the old *bureaux de charité*[168] under new conditions and a new name. This change of name is worth noticing however, for the importance attached to verbal distinctions was a marked revolutionary trait, and it might not be to consider too curiously to ask how far it represented a tendency to take words for things, *se payer de mots* in the French phrase. The decree that foundlings should no longer be foundlings, but "enfans naturels de la patrie[169]," and the substitution of "maison de santé" for "hôpital[170]," are instances. The word *char-*

---

[164]Hubert-Valleroux, "La Charité avant et depuis 1789 dans les Campagnes de France," p. 109.

[165]Taine, "Le Régime Moderne," p. 212. In Paris there were twenty hospitals left, out of thirty-four existing in 1790, with a revenue of 7,000 or 8,000 livres instead of over 8,000,000. Hubert- Valleroux, *loc. cit.*, p. 111.

[166]Law of 7 Frimaire, year II. See Maurice Block, "Dictionnaire de l'Administration Française," article "Bureau de Bienfaisance,"§1.

[167]Ravarin, "L'Assistance Communale en France," pp. 213, 215.

[168]See above, p. 28.

[169]By a decree of the Convention. Lallemand, "Histoire des Enfants Abandonnés et Délaissés," p. 257, note 1.

[170]Ravarin, "L'Assistance Communale en France," p. 32.

ity was especially disliked for its religious and political associations and was systematically avoided. The term "bureau de bienfaisance" coined by the abbé Saint Pierre[171], was discarded at the restoration, and replaced by the old name of "bureau de charité," but with Louis Philippe the revolutionary name came in again, apparently to stay.

Another sort of institution which was revived with the return of order was the work-house. This had existed in successive forms under the old régime—as the *hospices-ateliers* of Louis XIII, the *hôpitaux-généraux* of Louis XIV, the *maisons de correction* of Louis XVI. The Constituent Assembly had had its plans for a system of "maisons de répression," but did nothing. Napoleon[172], who hoped as fondly as Louis XIV to extirpate beggary and its train of related disorders by a system of work-houses and legal penalties, undertook to organize a complete preventive system[173]. A decree of July 5, 1808, ordered the establishment in every department of a *dépôt de mendicité* for *non-vagabond* beggars[174], and depots were accordingly organized on every hand during the next four years. With the fall of the emperor, however, the experiment was cut short, and of the comparatively small number of these institutions that have survived, the greater number are somewhat differently employed[175].

Though the elements of the new public assistance were thus much the same as those of the old, the whole had undergone a change. It was more definitely ordered, more consistent than the old and, whether for good or evil, more distinct from private charity. It was weaned from

---

[171]Ravarin, "L'Assistance Communale en France," p. 194.

[172]Napoleon, to quote his own words, "attachait une grande importance et une grande idée de gloire à détruire la mendicité." See Hubert-Valleroux, "La Charité avant et depuis 1789 dans les Campagnes de France," p. 246.

[173]See Gérando, "De la Bienf aisance Publique," III, 587 sq.; Granier, "Essai de Bibliographic Charitable," p. 43 sq.; Leroy Beaulieu, "L'Administration Locale en France et en Angleterre," pp.243-244; Block, "Dictionnaire de L'Administration Française," article "Mendiant." The consideration of Napoleon's system by Baron de Gérando is especially valuable, being the account not only of a competent observer and specialist, but of a man who was present at the discussions in regard to the suppression of the *dépôts de mendicité*.

[174]Tramps were to be sent to the *maisons de détention*. See Gérando, *loc. cit.*, p. 590.

[175]*Vide infra.*, p. 119.

49

the church, and took rank for the first time as a regular department of the administration[176]. It was under Napoleon that it received its modern shape, but he moulded it incidentally, almost unconsciously, as part of his work of social reconstruction, without any effort to create a systematic organization. The repression of beggary was the only part of the question in which he was personally interested. The measures of the 16 Vendémiaire and 7 Frimaire, year V, providing respectively for the establishment and administration of hospitals and of bureaux de bienfaisance, were before Napoleon's advent and were very meagre in their provisions. Nevertheless, they were almost the only laws on the subject until after the revolution of 1848, which forced attention to social questions. The new order owed very little to *legislation*; it was the work of administrative agencies, of ministerial circulars[177], of orders from the emperor, of the constructive processes which were at work making the France of to-day, and like the rest of the work of that wonderful epoch it has lasted with but comparatively slight changes through the eight political transitions which have since intervened[178].

---

[176]"C'est depuis 1789 que l'Assistance Publique entra parmi les services administratifs d'utilité générale et que l'Etat se crut obligé, dans une certaine mesure, de la réglementer." Leroy-Beaulieu, "L'Administration Locale en France et en Angleterre," p. 243.

[177]Hubert-Valleroux, "La Charité avant et depuis 1789 dans les Campagnes de France," p. 117.

[178]Ravarin, "L'Assistance Communale en France," p. 35.

Part II

The Modern Organization of Assistance in France.

It is not hard to distinguish two main principles which underlie French public assistance, and have always characterized it, more vaguely under the old regime, more distinctly, though not without exceptions, in modern times. In the first place it is as a rule voluntary, and not imposed on the community as an obligation; in the second place it is as a rule communal or local.

Voluntary Character of Public Assistance.

In regard to the voluntary character of public assistance the exceptions are more apparent than real. The parochial tax, which Francis I instituted in Paris, and which his successors tried to enforce throughout the kingdom[179], never took root, and even in those cities where it was nominally in force, was probably not exacted unless in times of special need[180]. Even the socialistic view of public assistance as a

---

[179] The *taxe des pauvres* was established in Paris in 1544, generalized throughout the kingdom by the ordinance of Moulins in 1566, and confirmed by an ordinance of May 22,1586, and by a declaration of June, 1642. It was sustained by numerous decisions of Parliament, especially by one bearing date December 30, 1740: "Toutes personnes et toutes communauté étaient tenues de contribuer au fonds des secours publics, *au sol pour livre des deux tiers des revenues qu'ils avaient daus la paroisse.*" The edict of 1656, after calling for voluntary subscriptions holds up the threat of forced contributions, "suivant les anciens reglemens." Parliament, however, in registering this edict modified it, to the effect that the citizens should be only invited to contribute without being liable to be taxed, unless in case of necessity.

Gérando, "De La Bienfaisance Publique," IV, 485-8. See also above, pp. 27, 34, 38, 43.

[180] As regards the probable execution of this tax I have found it difficult to get any information. The following passages give rather different impressions: "Beside the fact that these taxes were rare, they were found only in the cities, and almost wholly in some cities of the North of France, where the nearness of the Belgian provinces, where assistance had been made obligatory, afforded an example which was imitated. It was not, besides, an ordinary means of help, but a measure reserved for times of extreme need." Hubert-Valleroux, "La Charité avant et depuis 1789 dans les Campagnes de France," p. 20-21. Cf. also p. 61. Gérando, "De la Bienfaisance Publique," IV, 489, observes, "One is struck with the fact that these measures in regard to *droits des pauvres*, settlement, parochial responsibility, a special and unlimited tax and the mode of recovering it, although common to the two countries, have not occasioned in France the troubles, abuses, and complaints which have been so intense and so long continued in England. The reason of this singular phenomenon is that in France these measures have been carried out with more gentleness, regularity and restraint; it is because in France asylums and private institutions have afforded more abundant resources for the aid of the unfortunate." Gérando moreover

public debt, upheld by the revolution[181], had never led to any recognition of a right on the part of the pauper to demand aid and to recover his claim by legal means[182]. The abuses of the English poor-law were too present in men's minds[183].

In the reorganization that followed the revolution a return to legal charity was not dreamed of, and the old direct tax for the parish poor was not revived. The fear of over-legislation engendered by the work of the preceding years was strong, and, as has been said, no "lois d'ensemble" were passed on this subject. Malthus' essay, the French translation of which appeared in 1809, came to strengthen the opinion, even now rife in France, that the condition of England before

---

observes that the drawbacks of the poor tax have doubtless been lessened by the *haute tutelle administrative* or official supervision of charity, which, though mainly the work of Louis XIV, was established in principle in the legislation of Francis I, Henry II, Charles IX, Henry IV and Louis XIII. Ravarin, "L'Assistance Communale en France," p. 25, remarks that there was a tendency to replace the direct tax by *octroi* dues as easier to collect.

[181] It is curious to note that Montesquieu, writing in the middle of the eighteenth century, seems to commit himself to a distinctly socialistic view. "Alms given to a man naked in the streets do not fulfil the obligations of the state, which owes to all its citizens an assured livelihood, food, proper clothing, and a not unwholesome way of life," he says in his chapter on hospitals. ("Esprit des Lois" XXIII, 29.) He goes on to praise Henry VIII of England for having destroyed the convents which shelter the lazy, and concludes thus: "I have said that rich nations need hospitals because in them fortunes are subject to a thousand mischances, but it is evident that temporary aid would be better than permanent establishments. The trouble is a passing one and the help should be of the same nature and applicable to the particular case."

[182] "Jamais en France on ne reconnut à l'indigent une créance légale contre la société, jamais on n'a admit le droit à l'assistance." Leroy Beaulieu, "L'Administration Locale en France et en Angleterre," p. 241.

"La législation charitable en France est dominé par ce principe que, si la société a le devoir moral de ne laisser aucune souffrance réelle sans soulagement, l'assistance ne peut jamais être reclamée comme un droit par l'indigent." Report of M. Bucquet on the bureaux de bienfaisance, quoted by Block, "Dictionnaire de l'Administration Francaise," article "Assistance Publique."

[183] The English bug-bear had already begun to influence French legislators in the time of the Constituent Assembly. "Il est de la nature de toute taxe individuelle et dont l'assistance est l'object désigné, de s'augmenter même malgré l'opposition des contribuables...... C'est ici sortout que l'exemple de l'Angleterre nous est une grande leçon. La taxe des pauvres n'y était portée, au commencement du siècle, qu' à quinze millions, elle excède aujourd'hui soixante, et les contribuables, luttant sans cesse the contre son poids énorme, mais sentant l'impossibilité de la diminuer, se borneut à en modérer les progrès, sans aueun espoir de la jamais contenir. Outre les vices qu'offre une loi pareille .... elle nous découvre la plaie politique de l'Angleterre, et la plus dévorante, qu'il est également dangereux pour sa tranquillité et son bonheur de cicatriser ou de souffrir." See Monnier, p. 462 and Hubert-Valleroux, p. 85.

the poor law reform is the necessary result of allowing a legal claim to charity.

The numerous writers on charitable and social questions of the fourth and fifth decades of this century, when Dr. Villermé's report[184] on the conditions of life in the manufacturing centres of France had stirred the public conscience, are almost unanimous in the opinion that any intrusion of legal coercion is most hurtful[185].

The constitution of the second republic, nevertheless, reiterated the vague promises of general assistance made by the first, and, proclaiming the "droit à travail," proceeded to make its disastrous experiment with government workshops. This episode, result of complicated social and political movements, was of short duration, and the safer doctrine advocated by M. Thiers (in his report in the name of the "Comité d' Assistance Publique et de Prévoyance") was accepted. Yet the conception of public assistance as a public debt seems to make part of the inheritance of the republican form of government in France, and is not without influence at the present time[186]. The tendency to take a somewhat socialistic view of public charity, and to seek to make it almost a government monopoly by putting hindrances in the way of private iniative is, however, only a tendency, and is generally more than counteracted by the traditional horror of anything approaching the English system, by the dread of all state interference felt by the "economists," and by the jealousy of the Catholics who would like to keep charity as far as possible in the hands of the church.

Nevertheless, in behalf of two classes of unfortunates, the dangerously insane and particular categories of destitute children, certain obligations are imposed. The necessity for definite and reliable pro-

---

[184]"Tableau de l'Etat Physique et Moral des Ouvriers, employés dans les manufactures de coton, de laine et de soie." Paris, 1840.

[185]The most dogmatic opponent of the principle of obligation in charity is the Swiss pastor Naville in his much quoted "La Charité Legale," published in 1836. Baron de Gérando, whose classic treatise "De la Bienfaisance Publique" appeared three years later, is far more moderate in tone and possesses a breadth and practical insight which make his work very valuable.

[186]Cf. p. 166.

vision for these classes is obvious. The proper care of the first is as much a matter of police as of charity, while in regard to the "enfants assistés" the French Code[187], which forbids any attempt to fix the responsibility of fatherhood, affords a cogent reason for this exception, at least in so far as regards the illegitimate children, who are the great majority of the "enfants assistés." Yet even in these cases *"assistance can never be demanded as a right by the pauper,"* and on analysis the only actual legal obligation is seen to be that of the commune, which is required to contribute to the expenses of these two branches of assistance such a sum as the conseil général of the department shall determine. Though these two branches of assistance are, contrary to the general rule, organized by departments, the department, unlike the commune, is not *legally* bound to contribute. Its moral obligation to do so, however, never fails to be recognized.

Slight as is the legal element thus introduced, M. Léon Lallemand[188], sees in it[189] the cause of a neglect by voluntary benefactors of the branches of charity affected, and points out that of 16,000,000 francs spent for "assisted children" scarcely 350,000 came from private foundations in their favor, and that of this sum 300,000 at least was due to the generosity of former generations[190].

Among the contradictions to the general principle that assistance is voluntary should perhaps also be included the special taxes devoted

---

[187]Code civil, Art. 340, "La recherche de la paternité est interdite." The only exception is in case of rape. Compare Ravarin, "L'Assistance Communale en France," p268. This duty (i. e., that of providing for destitute children), "becomes a veritable obligation when the legislator refuses to the unmarried mother, deceived by a seducer or misled by her inexperience, the means of throwing the expenses of the child's education on the man. When the law makes itself the accomplice of such a denial of justice it is at least its duty to give the poor woman the help she cannot claim elsewhere."

[188]Author of the memoir on the history of foundlings, crowned by the Academy, and of various other works.

[189]In an article entitled "La Charité Legale en France," which appeard in the January numbers (January 1 and 16), for 1891, of the *Réforme Sociale*, the interesting organ of Le Play's Society of Social Economy.

[190]Compare with this the figures given by M. Bucquet for the bureaux de bienfaisance in 1871, an abnormal year unfortunately. Of the receipts of that year over forty per cent. was the income of real or personal property due mainly to former donations. Of the rest about a quarter came from the current charity of the year, while a sum half as great was received in the shape of bequests, etc.

to charity. They are not, however, of great importance. The most interesting is the *droit des pauvres, or taxe sur less spectacles*, to which allusion has been made before[191], and which has rather a curious history. The revolution abolished this tax, which was associated with the old regime, and the Directory, as has been said, restored it, setting it at a tenth for theatres and a fourth for other places of amusement. At first it was given entirely to the bureaux de bienfaisance, then the hospitals and asylums were allowed a share[192]. Where these are well endowed, however, the bureaus enjoy it as before. This tax has been criticised as a sumptuary measure and as interfering with the managers' profits, but the arguments against it have not much force, and it seems about as little objectionable as a tax can be. Formerly it was paid separately from the entrance fee at a special window and was the cause of some inconvenience, but now it is included in the price of the ticket, and most persons do not know that they are paying it[193].

Another special due for the benefit of the public assistance is paid in connection with the cemeteries, two-thirds of the sum paid for a lot going to the commune, one-third to the poor. The municipal council fixes, with the approval of the prefect, the rate to be paid for lots, and decides on the destination of the third belonging to the poor. In practice it is usually given to the bureaux de bienfaisance.[194]

---

[191] Cf. p. 72.

[192] The tax is at present one-tenth on the price of tickets in the case of theatres, daily concerts and some other amusements, one-quarter of the gross receipts in other cases. Curiously enough races do not come within the law, nevertheless they usually give part of their proceeds to the same fund. Entertainments given in aid of private charities are held to be subject to the tax, which being one-fourth of the gross receipts, *as estimated by the public authorities*, may swallow up or even exceed the profits. For a criticism of this see Hubert-Valleroux, "La Charité avant et depuis 1789 dans les Campagnes de France," pp. 284-5.

[193] For a full account of this tax consult Block, "Dictionnaire de l'Administration Française," article "Droit des Pauvres," and especially Ravarin, "L'Assistance Communale en France," pp. 213-225.

[194] Cf. Ravarin, "L'Assistance Communale en France," p. 225-227.

Communal Character of Public Assistance.

In regard to the second of the main traits of public assistance, namely its communal character, we find that this too, though subject to certain exceptions, is well marked. And yet the expression may be a misleading one to those accustomed to AngloSaxon ideas of local government, for French public charity has always been strongly centralized in its administration. It is communal in the sense that its organs, though corporations and largely autonomous, are more or less closely connected with the municipal administration, and serve, as a rule, only the commune in which they are situated. They are moreover, in principle, dependent upon the commune for their financial support in as far as it is not provided by their foundations or by private contributions. In reality the department and the state supply a not inconsiderable part of the funds[195].

The centralization in public assistance, though for the most part excessive according to our notions, has varied, as in all branches of French administration, with the political forms and theories of the times. In general it may be said to have passed through three phases since the revolution.

In the first, which was very brief, the experiment of decentralization was attempted, the local unit was strongly organized and the intrusion of the higher powers in local affairs restricted. At this time the directors of hospitals, asylums and bureaux de bienfaisance were remarkably independent of the central authorities and closely linked with the municipalities[196].

The second phase, inaugurated by Napoleon, was marked by intense concentration. Not only were the prefect and maire the creatures of the minister, even the members of the general and munici-

---

[195] Of the total expenses of public aesistance 4 per cent. are borne by the state, 16 per cent. by the departments, 15 per cent. by the communes omitting Paris, and 13 per cent. by Paris, while 52 per cent. is drawn from private sources, gifts and foundations. For the .sums see the table on p. 150.

[196] Ravarin, "L'Assistance Communale en France," p. 42

pal councils[197] were chosen by the government and kept under strict surveillance. The same influence dominated all branches of public charity[198].

The third phase is that in which the inevitable reaction made itself felt and produced more or less effectual efforts to decentralize, beginning under the July monarchy and accentuated by the events of 1848 and 1870[199]. As regards charitable administration this reaction has resulted in a moderate degree of decentralization, except for the capital and its department. The unique position of Paris has always made necessary special laws to regulate its assistance, but the system inaugurated in 1848, and which still obtains, is not only peculiar to it, but singularly opposed in spirit to that of the remainder of France, giving, as it does, the whole control of public assistance to a director of public assistance, who is appointed by the Minister of the Interior, and is almost independent of the municipal authorities, except as he is controlled by dependence on their appropriations[200].

With the endeavor to strengthen individual charitable institutions which has, in general, marked this third phase, has gone a progressive perfection of governmental inspection. Moreover, there has recently been added a board known as the Direction of Public Assistance, which acts as a sort of special council to the Minister of the Interior, the administrative chief of the service, and which introduces a new element of centralization, though of a different sort than the old[201].

In view of the importance of the effects of the degree of concentration on the working of the whole machinery, it may be well to take up more in detail the history of the powers of hospital commissions[202],

---

[197] The *conseil général* is the assembly of the department, the *conseil municipal* that of the commune, municipal rather than communal being in many cases the adjective to correspond to commune.

[198] Leroy Beaulieu, "L'Administration Locale en France et en Angleterre," p. 86.

[199] *Ibid*, p. 87.

[200] Ravarin, "L'Assistance Communale," p. 359 sq.

[201] Block, "Dictionnaire de l'Administration Française," article "Assistance Publique," 20. See also below, p. 163 sq.

[202] All the hospitals and asylums in a city are under the same commission unless in exceptional cases. Cf. Block, "Dictionnaire de l'Administration Française," article "Hopitaux et Hospices," 17.

as illustrating the development already given in general terms. According to the law of the sixteenth of Vendemiaire, year V[203], the municipal administration had the direct surveillance of the asylums in its district, appointing a board of five citizens, known as an administrative commission, to act as directors. The accounts of these commissions were submitted quarterly to the municipality before being sent up to the departmental authorities. A decree of the year XIII[204] wrought a complete change. The Minister of the Interior now appointed the commissioners with the advice of the prefect. The commune had nothing to do in the matter. But though composed only of government appointees the commission was entrusted merely with the carrying out of the government's views; not only had it no right to act in opposition to headquarters, it had not even the negative right to refuse to act.

When the Assembly of 1848 studied the question of public assistance, various projects were brought forward. M. Dufaure, the Minister of the Interior, wanted to see a complete reorganization, with a central board of administration, and local committees, and was strongly in favor of out-relief as opposed to relief in institutions[205]. No such reorganition was effected, however, and no agreement could be reached as to the hospital commissions, M. Dufaure being much opposed to the introduction of members elected by the municipal councils. The important law of August 7, 1851[206], which was the outcome of the discussion, put the power as regards public charity, as of other branches of the administration, into the hands of the prefects, but left the question of the hospital boards to be arranged by the executive, recommending, however, that the clergy should be represented in them, and that the board should not be allowed the "droit de presentation," which tended to make them close corporations. The latter suggestion only was followed in the decree of the next year, the prefect being

---

[203]Ravarin, "L'Assistance Communale en France," p. 42.

[204]Ravarin, "L'Assistance Communale en France," pp. 43, 52.

[205]For remarks as to his plans for *ateliers de charité*, see Hubert-Valleroux, "La Charité avant et depuis 1789 dans les Campagnes de France," p. 291 sq.

[206]Ravarin, "L'Assistance Communale en France," pp. 43 sq.

given the free nomination of the members. Their number was fixed at five as before, the maire to preside and have the casting vote, but as he was still, at that epoch, chosen by the government[207], this left little, if any, influence to the commune.

With the coming in of the third republic the subject was again discussed, but the most important alteration effected was that one member of the clergy of each religious sect recognized by the state[208] had a place in each commission[209]. A new law, passed in 1879, revoked this privilege on the ostensible ground that a fixed element was undesirable, though the strong anti-clerical bias of a large part of the dominant party suggests a more specific reason[210]. The commission, as at present constituted[211], consists of seven members—the maire, who presides, and six commissioners, two elected by the municipal council, and four appointed by the prefect. As regards the *tutelle administrative*[212], the commission of a hospital was, in 1851, at the same point as the municipal council, that is, both had then the negative right to refuse to act. Since then the communes have gone forward toward independence, but the hospital commissions have gained but little. The list of subjects, all matters of current administration, on which they can decide independently is strictly limited, and even as regards these decisions the prefect, the representative of the central executive, has a veto. In all other matters the prefect or municipal council must be consulted. Besides these means of control the hospitals are subject to yearly visits from the general inspectors, reporting to the Minister of the Interior, and also to the surveillance of the inspectors of finances.

What has been said of the hospital commissions is, for the most

---

[207]Since 1882, the maire is, except at Paris, elected by the municipal council by secret ballot and from among its own members. Block, "Dictionnaire de l'Administration Française," article "Organization Communale," §37.

[208]These are the Catholic, the Calvinist, the Lutheran and the Jewish. Block, *Ibid.*, article "Culte," 7.

[209]Ravarin, "L'Assistance Communale en France," p. 45.

[210]Cf. Ravarin, "L'Assistance Communale en France," p. 46.

[211]Ravarin, "L'Assistance Communale en France," p. 45.

[212]*Ibid.*, p. 53 sq.; Block, "Dictionnaire de l'Administration Française," article "Hopitaux et Hospices, 12 sq.

part, true of the bureaux de bienfaisance, although the reasons which justify interference in the case of hospitals and asylums seem wholly lacking in the case of the last[213].

In spite of this tendency toward centralization, French assistance is in general communal. Certain branches however, notably the care of assisted children and of the insane, are under the charge of the department. Certain functions again, and even the immediate management of certain asylums, belong to the state. In undertaking an account of the present constitution of public assistance I propose to classify it according to these divisions and to describe separately the charitable role of each of these agencies, the commune, the department and the state.

The Role of the Commune.

In the condition of the different communes of France there is the greatest possible difference; some are tiny primitive villages, if they can be called villages at all; others are great cities. Nevertheless. with the exception of Paris and Lyons, all have received the same organization, though one so elastic that it differs in reality as much as the local needs and resources.

Communal Resources.—

A few figures will help to give an idea of this diversity. The average extent ot a commune is a little over 1450 hectares[214], that is from thirty-five to thirty-six hundred acres, but this embraces such extremes as ten acres and over ninety thousand[215]. In population

---

[213]Ravarin,"L'Assistance Communale en France," 201-2; Leroy Beaulieu, "L'Administration Locale en France et en Angleterre", p. 245.

[214]A de Foville, "La France économique, statistique raisonnée et comparative," for 1889, p. 4.

[215]Arles, comprising La Crau and Camargue, has 103,000 hectares, or over 254,000 acres. *Ibid.*

and wealth the differences are even greater: in 1886 about half of the thirty-six thousand communes of France had 500 souls or less, seventy-four did not surpass fifty, all told. Forty-one were cities of more than 40,000 inhabitants[216]. The "ordinary receipts" of eighty-three per cent. of the communes ranged, in 1877, from $100 to $2,000, about two hundred communes had less. Nearly three hundred had more than $20,000, Paris had about $45,000,000[217].

Of the villages M. Emile Chevallier, in his book, "De l'Assistance dans les Campagnes,"[218] distinguishes two types—the village where "la grande industrie" is established, and the essentially agricultural. In the first, he says, the *"patron"* is almost always able to gather around him a laundry, day nurseries, benefit societies, a system of free medical treatment, hygienic houses, and, often, to obtain large grants from the commune or department for their maintenance. In a village where the people are farmers or engaged in small industries, such as hand-weaving, shoemaking, making brooms, glove-buttons, etc., a half or at least a third of the inhabitants are usually farmers, or vinedressers; the rest are day laborers, usually farm hands, sometimes artisans working at home or for wages, but all turning to farm work at certain seasons. Among these 50 per cent. at least usually have land of their own. Beside these there is a priest, sometimes a

---

[216]These facts are drawn from M. De Foville's figures, pp. 10-18, *loc. cit.*

[217]De Foville, pp. 487, 490. In each case I have given the "ordinary receipts" only, the proportion of the receipts classed as "extraordinary" varying greatly. In 1887 the total receipts of Paris were $60,000,000, of which $51,000,000 were "ordinary."

[218]This book is one of four written in response to an invitation of the Academy of Moral Sciences, which proposed for a competition the subject "L'Indigence et l'Assistance dans les campagnes depuis 1789." The first place was given to M. Hubert-Valleroux, who published his work, somewhat modified, as "La Charité avantet depuis 1789 dans les Campagnes de France, avec quelques exemples tirés de l'étranger." Paris, Guillaumin, 1890. M. Léon Lallemand, author of the excellent treatise on abandoned and neglected children, already referred to so often, came second with "De l'Assistance des Classes Rurales au XIX Siècle," published in 1889, also by Guillaumin. M. Chevellier's book, "De l'Assistance dans les Campagnes; Indigence, Prévoyance, Assistance" (Paris, Rousseau, 1889), was given the third place. The fourth competitor was M. Saunois de Chevert, whose "L'Indigence et L'Assistance dans les Campagnes depuis 1789 jusqu' à nos jours," Guillaumin, 1889, deals especially with institutions, both those in the city and in the country.

châtelain[219], and often one or two officials. This situation commonly leaves little place for poverty. It exists, however, here scattered, there more concentrated, according as the proportions given above change and the number of laborers increases. Charity is equally limited. There is a lack of initiative, any intermediary is distrusted, the press does not fill the place that it does in the city and the rich of the city do not give much in the country. In ordinary time there are few beggars, except in certain districts, as, for instance, in parts of Brittany, where old customs that still linger make beggary lucrative. The *cheminots*, tramps, who sometimes disturb the hamlets, come from the city not the country[220].

At the other end of the scale are the cities with large resources and larger claims upon their charity, where the conditions, though more complex, perhaps need less description as being more cosmopolitan. In all these different conditions one fixed legal element is the fact that a commune is not bound to make any local provision for the poor, the helpless or the sick. As a matter of fact in richer and more populous communes provision is of course made, to some extent at least. In communes of a simple sort it may very well happen that there is none at all. Sometimes there is simply a night-shelter put up for needy wayfarers, who might be dangerous guests in the farmers' barns. Where there is no regular bureau de bienfaisance there is sometimes a charitable commission to distribute help, which the municipal council may appropriate but cannot dispense directly[221].

The commune may also be said to grant aid when it grants exemption from taxation on the ground of poverty. As the sum to be paid by the commune is fixed, and what is taken from one man's burden is added to that of the others, this is really a form of communal assistance[222].

---

[219] That is a gentlemen with a country seat in the neighborhood.

[220] Chevallier, *loc.cit,* chapter VIII.

[221] Cf. Block, "Dictionnaire de l'Administration Française," Artiticle "Assistance Publique," § 17; and Ravarin, "L'Assistance Communale en France," p. 231. See also Chevallier, *loc. cit*, Chapter XIII.

[222] Block, "Dictionnaire de l'Administration Française," article "Contributions Directes." Cf. § 174.

Valuable resources for the poorer part of the population are in many communities furnished by the woods and commons[223] owned by the municipality, and though such resources can not strictly be called public assistance, they are in a sense nearly related to it, since it is often out of regard to the poor that the land is retained by the commune. Nearly one-ninth of the soil of France is in the hands of communes[224]; about one-third of the communes are the owners of woods amounting in all to almost a quarter of the wooded property of the country[225]. The administration of the communal woods may be assumed by the state under the forestry laws, or it may be left to the municipality. In the latter case they may be simply exploited for the general profit or given over to the inhabitants to use according to certain rules. Other communal lands may either be used in common, generally as pasture, or be divided among the householders in permanent or temporary allotments for which a payment may or may not be required. In one commune one household may even hold several lots, in case its members are inscribed on the "liste des indigents." In all these matters the municipal council has full jurisdiction, but the real regulator is immemorial custom. Besides these more important communal rights of wood-cutting, pasture, or communal holdings, there are certain trifling privileges[226], such as the right to gather wild fruits or fatten swine in the forest which, slight in themselves, are yet precious aids

---

[223] Peat and seaweeds also furnish in certain districts important additions to communal wealth.

[224] In 1882, 4,621,450 hectares, 8.74 per cent. of the French territory. De Foville, "La France Economique," p. 67.

[225] Eleven or twelve thousand communes own nearly 2,000,000 hectares in woods. De Foville, *loc. cit.*, p. 182.

[226] The legal technicalities of these old communal privileges are very curious. *La cucittelte* is the distinctive name of the gathering wild fruits, etc. *Affouage* is the right to cut wood for fuel. It is very carefully regulated by law. *Maronage* is the right to wood for building and repairs. *La glandêe* is the privilege of letting swine into the forest to feed on acorns. When they feed also on beechnuts and other fruits this is called *panage*. *La paisson* is the right to pasture animals on land coming under forestry jurisdiction. The *vaine pâture* is the right to send cattle, etc., separately or in a herd, to pasture on the private fields of the inhabitants of the commune after harvest or when they are lying fallow, provided, always, they are not enclosed. For all this matter consult Block's "Dictionnaire de l'Administration," article "l'Organisation Communale," especially § 264-265. See also articles on "Forêts," "Affouage," "Varech," "Tourbières."

in a country where land has a high value and thrift is carried to its utmost point[227]. Another right accorded by the law is that of gleaning after the harvest has been gathered in, and after the sun has set. The poor only are allowed the privilege, and usually a card signed by the maire and certifying the indigence of the bearer is required[228].

Besides these very primitive forms of public charity (or of limited communism, as we choose to consider them), every commune in France profits, if the need arises, by the institutions for the insane and for foundlings organized by the department. Every commune, too, is assessed for a certain share of the expenses of the latter service, regardless of whether it has benefited by it or not; but the general council of the department takes into account, in apportioning the shares, the ability of the communes to pay, and may even excuse those communes that are too poor. As regards the insane the communes are responsible only for the dangerously insane who have acquired their settlement (*domicile de secours*) in the commune by birth or by a year's residence, and then for only a certain part of the expenses. varying with the resources of the municipality. Communes having 100,000 francs a year or more pay not more than one-third, those with less than 5,000 pay one-sixth or less and may be wholly excused. If a commune wishes to have a pauper, who is harmlessly insane, received in the departmental asylum, it may be called on for a larger share, but not for more than half at most. If the *domicile de secours* of a dangerous lunatic is doubtful the department is bound to take charge of him[229].

---

[227] Sometimes, however, communal property, and especially the right to gather fire-wood, proves so attractive to the poor as to draw them to a commune, in which case it is anything but a benefit to the commune. Hubert-Valleroux, "La Charité avantet depuis 1789 dans les Campagnes de France," p. 143. See also p. 76 for an interesting paragraph on common land.

[228] Block, "Dictionnaire de l'Administration Française," article "Glanage."

[229] Cf. Ravarin, "L'Assistance Communale en France," V, IV, and VI, IV.

Hospitals and Asylums.—

Outside of these two classes for which provision is assured, the opportunities of asylum for the sick and helpless poor are rather precarious and especially so in the country communes. In 1889 there were in all 1,679 hospitals and asylums—308 hospices[230], 489 hospitals, 882 mixed establishments. Comparing with this number the 2,185 which the Comité de Mendicité (Report 7, p. 5[231]) reported, affirming that the list was not complete, we see that the asylums and hospitals are not yet as many in France as before the revolution. It is likely, however, that there are as many or more places available, for there are more large institutions, and fewer of the little old foundations supplying perhaps only three or four beds. These often dated from the days of plague and leprosy when such small hospitals, dotted through the countryside, in isolated places for fear of contagion, were both common and much needed. As the special call for them disappeared and the lust for great institutions was developed, these—whether through the mere decay of time or through direct abolition, such as Louis XIV practised—largely disappeared and their place has not been supplied[232].

The large asylums of to-day are mainly in or near cities, where the need and the means are both so great, and the country regions are sparsely supplied. The greater part of the asylums of France are private foundations, often very ancient. They are administered by a board of directors, partly appointed, partly elected, as has been described[233]. They are incorporated bodies and hold property, often

---

[230]In common speech any asylum is called an *hospice*, but an *hospice* properly speaking is for the old, the infirm, children, etc., and not, like the *hôspital*, for the sick. An *hôspital-hospice* receives all these classes. See Chevallier, "De l'Assistance dans les Campagnes," Introduction.

[231]Cf. Hubert-Valleroux, "La Charité avant et depuis 1789 dans les Campagnes de France," p. 173.

[232]On January 1, 1869, according to an official inquiry presented in that year by M. Bosredon, there were in France 1557 hospitals or *hospices*; of these 757 were in towns *chefs lieux* of cantons, only 281 were in rural communes. See Saunois de Chevert, "L'Indigence et L'Assistance dans les Campagnes depuis 1789 jusqu' à nos jours,"

[233]See above, p. 84 sq.

possessing considerable real estate, beside other property, chiefly in government securities[234].

"Sickness," it has been said, "confers settlement," by which it is meant that any hospital not devoted to a special class of cases is required to admit, within the limits of its resources, any person falling sick in the commune, whether a regular inhabitant of the commune or not[235]. It is not, however, obliged to receive persons from other communes, and not one commune in fifty, probably, has a hospital of its own, so that there is much complaint of lack of hospital accommodation for the country population. Nevertheless, a large part of the places in the existing hospitals are always empty—24,562 out of a total of 59,997 in 1878[236]. This is partly due to places being reserved for the needs of the army, but for the most part it is the result of the narrow policy often adopted in regard to admission. Beside the waste implied in this large proportion of vacant beds, it entails disproportionate expense upon the patients, who have the general expenses to bear among them.

Various attempts have been made to rectify this state of things. A law of 1851 inaugurated a system meant to bring the departments, the hospitals and the communes into cooperation. According to this plan the general council of a department divides its territory into a number of "rural districts" and designates a hospital to serve for each, the hospital being expected to set aside a certain number of places

---

[234] In the last century the authorities, beginning with Chancellor D'Aguesseau, with an edict of 1749, brought considerable pressure to bear to prevent the increase of property held in mainmorte, and to make the hospitals convert their real estate into government securities, greatly to the advantage of the government finances. Necker was even anxious to employ coercion and was vexed with the king that he would not consent. After the restoration of the property confiscated from the hospitals during the revolution, the policy pursued was simply to encourage its investment in *rentes* on the state. In 1858 M. Espinasse, Minister of the Interior, undertook to force this policy upon the hospitals, but he was not sustained in his attempt. Since then it has not been urged by the government. It is nevertheless the tendency of managers of hospitals to pursue this course. As the value of real estate is on the rise and that of money and personal property falling, such conversion of real estate is permitted by the authorities only on condition of a certain capitalization. See Monnier, pp. 242-248; Ravarin,"L'Assistance Communale en France," pp. 83-87.

[235] Ravarin,"L'Assistance Communale en France, "p. 159.

[236] Investigation of 1878, quoted by M. Cheysson, "L'Assistance Rurale Intercommunale," *Réforme Sociale*, September 15, 1886, p. 279.

at a moderate price for the use of the communes of its district and giving the use of its buildings free.

The communes which accept this arrangement pay, at the rate agreed upon, for any patients which they may send to the hospital, and the department comes to the aid of the communes that find this too heavy a burden. Nothing is obligatory, and the scheme has not been as widely adopted as was hoped[237]. The distance to the hospital is often too great to admit of transporting the sick, and the caution, to call it by no harsher name, of the country population is averse to committing the commune to the expense without being sure of the support of the department. In practice the hospital, as far as its resources allow, usually admits urgent cases without inquiring too closely into their place of origin or the prospect of future repayment[238]. The admission into the hospices is much more rigidly regulated than admission into hospitals, though in other respects there are few differences to note. Each governing board makes its own requirements as regards age and settlement, according to the means of the establishment and the demands upon it, and decides upon each case. The hospices receive two classes of inmates, those that are literally paupers and those that

---

[237] Cf. Ravarin, "L'Assistance Communale en France", p. 158 sq.

[238] At least so says Ravarin, *loc. cit.*, p. 160-1. It is said that the neighbors of a sick man will sometimes carry him by night to the doors of the nearest hospital, and leave him there, thus forcing the hands of the managers, who can hardly leave him there to die. For accounts of the difficulty in procuring admission and the red tape involved, see Cheysson, "L'Assistance Rurale Intercommunale," *Réforme Sociale*, September 15, 1886, and October 1, 1886, p. 479-480 and *passim*, and Hubert-Valleroux, "La Charité avant et depuis 1789 dans les Campagnes de France," p. 177, p. 182 and *passim*.

A point worth alluding to, though it cannot be entered on here, is the attendance of sisters of charity in hospitals and asylums. It is common for a board of directors to enter into an agreement with some religious community to secure the services of its members, paying a certain amount to the community and providing for the maintenance of those in service. Such treaties stipulate that the sisters shall be treated "as daughters of the house, and not as mercenaries," and that in temporal matters they shall owe obedience to the directors. See Ravarin, "L'Assistance Communale en France," p. 64 sq., p. 68. The question of the employment of *réligieuses* by the public assistance is one that naturally enlists strong feelings on both sides and is the cause of much bitterness. Paris has established schools for lay nurses, men and women, at two of her asylums. For an unfavorable criticism of the sisters, see a little volume, "Paris Municipal," by Leneveux, in the "Bibliothèque Utile," published by Félix Alcan. See p. 82 sq. De Goncourt's story of "Soeur Philomène" gives a beautiful picture of a hospital sister.

own something, though not enough to live on. The admission of these latter in return for what they can give, while not so great a burden on the establishment, is often quite as valuable an aid as that given to paupers, and probably helps a more worthy class. As far as possible separate quarters are provided for those that have paid something[239].

As a general rule old age cases are not admitted until after 70, and the law does not permit a commune which has no asylum to have its cases of this class admitted to that of another commune. The country districts are, therefore, for the most part, obliged to provide for the old by outdoor relief alone. This is precisely the intention of the legislator, the idea being that in a rural community it is demoralizing to send the old to an institution; that families, while ready to throw off the burden if possible, can and should care for their own old people and invalids with, perhaps, a little aid from the bureaux de bienfaisance[240]. The case is different in the city, where the natural relations are often broken and cases of isolation frequent, and where, moreover, the expense of housing a useless inmate is much greater. Moreover the country populations still retain a great horror of the "hospice," which it is perhaps well not to too much mitigate.

This dislike of asylums is felt not only by the people, but by French thinkers on these subjects. Whereas the English theory has been that out-relief tends strongly to pauperize its recipients, on whom it entails no hardship and sets no mark, while an asylum will be resorted to only in dire extremity, the French idea has been that the entire relief of the family and friends from any further responsibility, when once their charge had been admitted into an asylum, is demoralizing and likely to lead to abuses; while a little assistance at home, given as far as possible in kind, would prevent extreme suffering or help to tide over on a crisis, without loosening the natural bonds or leading to carelessness and relaxed efforts[241].

---

[239]Cf. Block, "Dictionnaire de l'Administration Française," art., "Hopitaux et Hospices," § 57-59.

[240]Cf. Ravarin, "L'Assistance Communale en France" p. 180.

[241]See Block, "Dictionnaire de l'Administration Française," art., "Hopitaux et Hospices," § 67, 68.

In pursuance of this idea, the asylums are allowed and encouraged to devote part of their funds to out-door relief. This is quite contrary to the usual principle that funds must be used strictly for the object designated. The part that can be thus employed by asylums was at first set at one fifth of their revenue, then raised in 1873 to one-quarter, or even to a possible third, to be employed in cooperation with bureaux de bienfaisance for the treatment of the sick in their homes, and for yearly allowances to the old or helpless kept with their families[242]. The inquiry in regard to hospitals and asylums undertaken in 1864 showed that fifty-six asylums, whose average income was only about $365 a year, did nothing but give out-relief; others—more than a third of the whole number—gave in this way something over $1,000,000, or about a sixth of the sum given by the bureaux de bienfaisance which are the regular organs of out relief.

Bureaux de Bienfaisance.

—The original plan when bureaux de bienfaisance were instituted in 1798 was to have at least one such bureau in every commune, but this was found to be quite impracticable[243], and only 40 per cent. of the communes of France, and these for the most part the most populous, now possess a bureau[244].

Bureaux de bienfaisance adapt themselves to every condition, and, useful in direct proportion to their resources, require no preliminary outlay, so that it would seem that they should rise in response to the need for them with a promptness which cannot be expected in the

---

[242]Cf. M. Cheysson's remarks in a paper on "L'Assistance Rurale Intercommunale." "Le secours à domicile qui est, à notre sens, de toutes les formes de secours, la plus féconde, la plus humaine, et la plus économique. L'assisté reste ainsi dans sa famille, au milieu de ses habitudes, et loin d'être une charge pour les siens, il leur apporte un peu de bien-étre, dont il ressent le contre coup en soins affectueux et empressés." *La Réforme Sociale*, October 1, 1886, p. 362; compare also Ravarin, "L'Assistance Communale en France" p. 399.

[243]Block, "Dictionnaire de l'Administration Française," article "Bureaux de Bienfaisance."

[244]The communes of France numbered 36,121 in 1886. The bureaux de bienfaisance were 14,574 in 1885. The population of the districts provided with bureaux is 22,000,000 out of the 38,153,000 in France (figures of 18851. See De Foville, "La France Economique," pp. 16, 66, 9.

case of costly institutions. Though they are usually due to private generosity it is not unheard of for a commune to make the foundation from its municipal resources, a thing which seldom happens in the case of other charitable establishments outside of large cities. However founded, a government authorization is necessary to the creation of a bureau de bienfaisance as of any other incorporated body. It is considered bad policy to create a bureau not assured of at least 50 francs annual income, apart from private gifts, municipal grants, etc[245]. Nevertheless in 1871, out of a total of 13,367 bureaus, 644 were idle for want of means, and 1,062 more had not more than 50 francs of "ordinary receipts" a year, counting under that head the municipal grants, etc., just excluded.

As might be expected, the number of bureaus has increased steadily, a fact shown by a comparison of the results of the three official inquiries of which they have been the subject. These were undertaken, one by M. De Gasparin in 1833, one by Baron de Watteville in 1847 and one by M. Paul Bucquet in 1871. Unfortunately each of these important investigations was made under exceptional circumstances, which somewhat impair their value. In 1833 the bureaux de bienfaisance numbered 6,275, in 1847, 9,336, in 1871, 13,367. In 1884 the number of bureaus in active operation had grown to 14,760[246].

The bureau de bienfaisance is an incorporated body (*personne civile*), as are also hospitals and asylums, and it is therefore capable of holding property and receiving legacies. It also holds the unique position of legal representative of the poor, so that its president, the maire, is alone allowed to accept any legacy left in general terms to the poor, and for it alone can public collections, etc., be taken up[247].

The composition and powers of its governing body, the *commission administrative*, have already been described[248].

---

[245] Ravarin, "L'Assistance Communale en France," pp. 193-200.

[246] Loua, "La France Sociale et Economique," 1888, p. 17. In the period between 1833 and 1871, the *bureaux* increased 113 per cent.; the persons helped by them, 130 per cent.; their resources, 208 per cent.; the population of France, 11 per cent.

[247] For a fuller discussion of this see later p. 169 sq.

[248] Cf. p. 87 *et ante*.

The character of a bureau necessarily varies with the community in which it is situated and its own resources. According to the investigation of M. Bucquet, in 1871, there were 1,506 bureaus spending between one and fifty francs a year, 7,424 spent 500 francs or less, 644 had nothing to give and 352 more gave nothing. At the same time the twenty bureaus of Paris averaged 239,915 francs each. Obviously no general description can be given which will fit such diverse institutions. The country bureau is practically a relief fund, generally due, originally, to some private bequest and eked out with a grant from the commune and certain legal perquisites, and administered by an official board. In Paris each arrondissement has its bureau de bienfaisance, with as many maisons de secours as may be necessary. In these the numerous staff of employees is lodged and applicants are seen, relief and medicine dispensed, meetings held, and bed-linen and other necessaries, kept for that purpose, loaned on occasion. Each arrondissement is divided into "zones," each under the care of one director.

A decree of August 12, 1886, met a long-felt want by providing consistent regulations for the Paris bureaus, and its provisions may be taken as typical of the bureau in its most developed form[249]. In addition to the board of managers, whose number may be as many as eighteen, and whose services are unpaid, there are, attached to the bureaus, doctors selected by competitive examination, *sages femmes*, *commissaires* or agents, and employees for other less important duties, such as clerks, etc[250]. There are beside *dames de charité*, elected by the managers but rendering their services gratuitously, to visit the sick, distribute relief and otherwise assist.

"Annual aid" is given only to persons of French nativity, with a "settlement" in Paris, and either over 65, orphaned and under 13, or suffering from a chronic infirmity or sickness. Those so helped

---

[249] For a vivid if somewhat antiquated picture of the Paris bureau de bienfaisance and the incidents of its work, cf. Maxime du Camp, "Paris Ses Organes, Ses Fonctions et SaVie," p. 123-141.

[250] It is common for bureaux de bienfaisance, as well as for hospitals, to enter into agreements with religious orders for the services of the sisters of charity. See p. 96, note 2.

are required to tell what, if any, aid they receive elsewhere, under pain of being struck off the list. The names of those receiving aid are communicated to societies which will reciprocate. The list of pensioners is revised carefully each year.

"Temporary aid" can be given in case of temporary need, especially in cases of sickness and confinement. The name, address, business and date of cessation of relief are to be registered in every case.

Bureaus are also allowed to grant "special aid" for expenses for traveling home (*frais de voyage et rapatriement*), rent, apprenticeship, and admission into orphan asylums, sanitariums, etc., or into mutual benefit societies.

To decide ordinary cases a provisional committee meets weekly, and the board at certain stated periods, but the president and doctors can act at once in urgent cases. At the annual meeting all the force are present and the report for the year is read.

Such are some of the rules laid down for the conduct of the Paris bureaus. Elsewhere the drawing up of rules as to admission to relief, etc., is one of the most important duties of the board of managers. It is, like all their other acts[251], subject to the approval of the prefect.

To understand the situation and work of the bureaux de bienfaisance throughout the country' we must turn to M. Bucquet's report of 1871[252] already quoted from.

In that year the total of the "ordinary" receipts was between twenty-six and twenty-seven million francs. Deducting the receipts of the Paris bureaus from property and from municipal grants, etc., which cannot be classified, we find that 48 per cent. was the returns from invested property (some six thousand francs from government securities and four thousand from real estate, with another thousand from other investments), and that nearly 17 per cent. was due to current charity, making 65 per cent. due in the main to voluntary gifts. 26

---

[251] In some cases the sub-prefect decides. Cf. Ravarin, "L'Assistance Communale en France," p. 206-207.

[252] Bucquet, Paul, "Enquête sur les Bureaux de bienfaisance. Documents recueillis par les Inpecteurs génèraux des Etablissments de bienfaisance et rapport au Ministre sur la situation des bureaux de bienfaisance en 1871." Paris, *Imprimerie National*, 1874.

per cent. was due to municipal grants, 1 per cent. to state grants, .02 per cent. to departmental grants and .07 per cent. to special taxes and perquisites, or, together, decidedly less than a third from these sources.

In regard to the property held by the bureaus it is to be remarked that soon after their creation they were given, beside the scanty proceeds of the tax on amusements, certain prerevolutionary foundations or what remained of them. It is nevertheless true that the bulk of their endowment is due to modern generosity. From 1845 to 1874 they received in gifts or legacies thirteen or fourteen millions of francs, about a quarter of it in the shape of real estate[253].

In regard to municipal grants it must be said that of the five or six millions to which they amount in all[254] most is absorbed by a comparatively small number of rich communes. Out of 13,367 bureaus only 2,498 receive municipal aid.

The matter of municipal grants is complicated with a controversy in regard to the *octroi* or city dues. This form of tax was common under the old regime but was abolished in 1791. In the year VII (1800-1), it was reestablished, first in Paris where the asylums were in need of funds, then in other cities, under the name of *octroi municipal et de bienfaisance*. The proceeds of the duties thus imposed were at first devoted primarily to charity, of which there was then great need, and secondarily to the general needs of the commune. This tax has, however, commonly become, and notably in Paris, the chief purveyor of the necessary city funds. It has been contended by certain authorities that this is an abuse. Baron Dupin even went so far as to maintain that the word *et* in the name of the tax was an interpolation, and that it was "properly to be known as octroi *municipal de bienfaisance.*"[255] However this may be, the fact is that the sum contributed to public charities by communes enjoying an *octroi* is in general a very small

---

[253]In 1881 the incomes from endowments amounted to fourteen million, an increase of nearly fifty per cent. over that of ten years before.

[254]Beside the Parisian grants.

[255]See his "Histoire de l'Administration des Secours Publics." See Granier, "Essai de Bibliographie Charitable," p. 109, p. 447.

part of the receipts of the tax.

Next in importance to the bureaus, after their own revenue and the grants of the commune, are the proceeds of private charity which they are authorized and expected to solicit in various ways, such as by house- to-house collections, by setting up a box (*tronc*) in churches and other public buildings, and by taking up church collections (to be arranged with the ecclesiastical authorities.)[256] According, however, to the statistics of M. Bucquet for the year 1871 only a small proportion of the then existing bureaus made any use of these means of collecting money. But it must be remembered that a considerable number of those claiming an official existence were practically dead, and that others, endowed by a liberal founder, enjoyed a sufficient income without such support. Others again were in communities too poor to give, or too well off to need help—or how else shall we interpret the not inconsiderable number of bureaus having a certain revenue but spending nothing?

Besides the sources of income already spoken of and the supplementary grants sometimes allowed by the state or a department, the bureaus enjoy certain *droits attribués*, the two chief of which, the tax on theatres and a share of the proceeds of cemeteries, have been already described[257]. The sum to be derived from these is small; it might, nevertheless, be of much assistance to needy bureaus, and the great carelessness of the municipal authorities in this regard seems much to be regretted. In 1871 only 3,750 bureaus out of 13,367 drew any benefit from these rights. Other dues (chiefly fines, such as those for infractions of the law in regard to unhealthy lodgings), which go to public charity, are practically insignificant.

Of these different classes of receipts all, except those from "troncs, quêtes et collectes," are enjoyed by the hospitates and asylums as well by the bureaux de bienfaisance. The latter, however, are without certain sources of income which belong to hospitals and asylums, viz.: certain successorial rights, which are more curious legally than im-

---

[256]For the privileges of the bureau in these matters see p. 169 sq.
[257]Cf. pp. 80-82.

portant practically, certain contributions from the monts de *piété*, of which I will speak later, and, finally, the considerable sums received both by hospitals and asylums from paying inmates[258].

The expenditure of the bureaux de bienfaisance is mainly in direct relief and is in very large part for food. The smallest among them, and there were in 1871 more than 1500 spending only between one and fifty francs, confine themselves to giving food. It is laid down as general rule that relief shall be given as far as possible in kind, which means often in *bons*, or tickets, good for a certain amount of meat, coal, medicine or what not. Much even of what is entered on the books as money aid is, in reality, laid out in purchases by the agents or Sisters of Charity. The sums given directly are very small. Of 32,362 gifts of money made in cases of sickness in Paris, 13,680 were of from three to five francs, and the average was 4.09 francs.

Taking the 301 largest bureaus, those spending 10,000 francs or over, we find a total expenditure of some 16,000,000 francs, of which nearly 10,000,000 goes for relief in kind. This sum includes 7,700,000 for food (bread, wine, meat, etc.); 900,000 for *fourneaux économiques;*[259] 660,000 for clothing, bedding and laundry work; 570,000 for fuel and 21,000 for dresses for first communions.

The next largest outlay, not quite 1,700,000, is for money aid, of which some 200,000 goes for rent.

Setting aside "administrative" expenses, including wages, the most

---

[258]Cf. Ravarin, "L'Assistance Communale en France," pp. 141-8, and 208-233.

[259]That is kitchens where cheap but nourishing food may be had, either to eat on the spot or to carry away. The first experiment with these *fourneaux* was made in Paris at the beginning of this century in connection with a bureau de bienfaisance. At that time almost the only dish offered was the soup, known by his name, which Benjamin Thompson, Count Rumford, invented for his poor in Munich. During the second empire these kitchens were under the special patronage of the Prince Imperial, but it was during the siege of Paris that they were most appreciated. They were also invaluable during the excessively cold season of 1879-'80, when seventeen new ones were created, for which the public assistance at once took 100,000 *bons*. In the same year the government allowed these tickets to be put on sale at tobacconists' shops where they are still procurable. There are at present (1890-'91) twenty-nine *fourneaux* in Paris supported by the Société Philanthropique and served by Sisters of Charity. A very interesting account of them is given in the first of a delightful series of papers on French charities that appeared in the New York *Herald*, in the issues of February 14, March 7 and April 25, 1891.

next important expense is for medical assistance, including doctors, nurses, medicines, apparatus, etc., and amounting to about 1,500,000 francs for the 301 bureaus.

For allowances to orphans, to the aged and for providing wet nurses 600,000 francs was spent. The items classed as "moral and preventive" cover a wide range, some objects being provided for by certain bureaus, others by others. Thus fifty-two bureaus were supporting or helping schools, ten interested themselves in promoting apprenticeship, eleven were giving to asylums for the aged, or to *depôts de mendicité*, or to *ateliers de charité*[260] and other ways of providing employment. Dowries and trousseaux as rewards for good conduct (presumably drawn from a special bequest), day nurseries and aid to released prisoners also figure in the list. The total expense of this class of relief is however less than 400,000, even if to it be added the subsidies granted to other agencies of relief, such as the "service de la médicine gratuite," or to charitable societies. The proportionate amount of this sort of outlay would, of course, be less in the other and smaller bureaus, but it must be remembered, on the other hand, that 1871 was an abnormal year in which the needs of the moment were exceptionally pressing and organizations of all sorts were thrown into more or less disorder.

M. Bucquet does not confine himself to statistics, but discusses the function and efficacy of the bureau de bienfaisance very frankly.

"Their very limited means," he says, "allow them to give only meagre relief. They are prevented from doing all the good they

---

[260]Though *ateliers de charité* (i. e., usually, out-door employments such as roadmaking) seem to be losing ground as a mode of public assistance, much interest is now taken by private agencies in *l'assistance par le travail* and in experiments along this line, in the agricultural colonies of Holland, the laborer's colonies and stations of Germany, and the woodyards and refuges in the United States and England, both those of the Salvation Army and others. The interest in the efforts of other countries, and the desire to transplant whatever seems desirable are very marked in France at the present time, and have doubtless been stimulated by the numerous international congresses held of late years and notably by the Congrès d'Assistance which met at Paris in 1889. For accounts of experiments now making in France with organized charity, *l'assistance par le travail*, etc. see notices scattered through the journal *La Réforme Sociale* during the last few years.

would, and it is only exceptionally that they can attempt to rescue a needy family or a deserving individual from poverty by means of aid of any considerable amount. But we must not conclude from this that the assistance given by the bureau is ineffectual and useless. The permanent assistance given to the old man, the temporary allowance made to the ablebodied when overtaken by sickness or loss of employment is certainly not large, but increased by the gifts of private charity it makes life less haid, the crisis of the moment less painful. To judge the charitable action of the bureaux de bienfaisance we must not isolate them; on the contrary, we must complete them by grouping around them the societies of "maternal charity," the day nurseries, the state provision for assisted children, the asylums and hospitals, the "national institutions," the gratuitous medical treatment for the poor in the country, the benefit societies, the monts de piété, the society for the extinction of beggary and all the numerous and active forms of private charity which, adding their help to that of the bureaux de bienfaisance, leave, so to speak, no suffering without relief, no misery without help."

Much less cheerful is the view of the subject taken by Maxime DuCamp in his account of public charity in Paris, already referred to[261].

"I have," he says, "accompanied the visitors in their expeditions, and I have come back with an impression which it is very hard to precisely define. The poverty which I have seen is frightful, but it is in the main superficial. Certainly this is to be rejoiced at, but how can one help being irritated at the thought that it is in most cases the result of precocious debauch, of laziness, of ill regulated appetites, and that the money that is asked for and that will be given is almost always spent at the cabaret. Does this mean that we must check our generosity and cease to give? By no means; if one in a hundred thousand gifts succeeds in bringing relief and really doing good that is enough; charity has not been in vain, and it has not

---

[261] "Paris, Ses Organes, Ses Fonctions, et Sa Vie," IV, 145.

been lacking. But why trouble oneself with the question of utility ? It is from self-respect and in the abstract that we must be benevolent; a good action which finds its reward elsewhere than in the conscience of the benefactor at once becomes inferior. In this respect the visitors deserve great praise, they do good with the profound conviction, formed by a long experience, that they shall not obtain any lasting results. Behind the poverty they see very clearly the vice that has caused it, but they remember only one thing—the poverty that they have found and that must above all be helped. In hundreds of reports I have read "What can be given will do no good and will be at once spent in debauch, but the poverty is such that help is necessary?""

It is such ideas as these that have brought the name of charity into reproach. Assuredly they are less common to-day than they were twenty years or more ago when this was written, but to believe that they were ever characteristic of its best exponents would be to overlook the work of such men as De Gérando, La Rochefoucauld-Liancourt and others akin to them.

The Public Assistance of Paris.-—

Before closing this account of the part taken by the commune in public assistance, it will be necessary to speak of some of the peculiarities of the system as seen in Paris, where the organs of assistance are the same as in the provincial communes, only further developed, but where its administration is exceptional in various important points.

From the earliest time the capital has been the object of special charitable legislation, as has been abundantly shown in the account of charity under the old regime. During the most terrible days of the revolution a *commission de bienfaisance*, instituted by the municipality, did its best to relieve the misery of those dreadful times. After the creation of the bureaux de bienfaisance by the law of the year V, a reorganization took place; indoor and out-door relief were made independent of one another, and the latter was put under the charge of forty-eight bureaus—one for each of the "sections" into which the city was then divided—with a central bureau, under the Minister of the Interior, at their head[262].

In the year IX a new system was tried which was in vigor throughout the first half of this century. Bureaux de bienfaisance, hospitals and asylumns were put, together, under the charge of a council with legislative functions, and a commission of salaried officials charged with the executive duties. This division of powers was not, however, observed in practice and great confusion ensued[263]. The events of 1848 helped to inaugurate a change, and the law of January 10, 1849, established the system which still obtains. To a *Directeur de l'Asistance publique de Paris*, appointed by the Minister of the Interior, is given both the direction and execution of all that pertains to the public charity of the capital. He is, indeed, assisted by a *conseil de surveillance*, whose members, appointed by the president on the minister's nomination, are supposed to represent the different interests involved, but its functions are purely consultative and it has no right to trammel the action of the Director[264].

Neither has the municipal council any direct voice in the management of the public assistance. It votes, however, nearly half the funds[265], and though it is contended that this grant is obligatory, on account of the terms on which the city *octroi*[266] is allowed, its amount depends largely on the good will of the municipal council and this fact lends a certain weight to its views[267].

Under this system indoor and outdoor relief are united[268], but the

---

[262] See a little book published by Guillaumin & Cie. in 1849, "Du Paupérisme et Des Secours Publics dans la Ville de Paris, par M. Vee, maire du 5e arrondissement de Paris," p. 23.

[263] Ravarin, "L'Assistance Communale en France," p. 358 sq.

[264] Ravarin, "L'Assistance Communale en France," p. 359.

[265] Ravarin, *loc. cit.*, pp. 361, 365-366.

[266] See above, p. 104.

[267] Ravarin, however, says of the conseil municipal, "il ne saurait, sans excéder ses pouvoirs, tracer au Directeur de l'Assistance publique des règles de conduite, ni subordonner le vote des crédits à l'accomplissement de ses prescriptions." *Loc. cit.*, pp. 366.

[268] In 1870 a break was made and outdoor relief was for a short time a mu-

agents of the latter, the bureaux de bienfaisance, retain a degree of individuality not accorded the latter. They are *personnes civiles* and capable therefore of receiving bequests, and they have their own boards headed by the maire of the arrondissement[269]. It is, however, from the "Assistance Publique" that they receive their funds, outside of special gifts—their shares of the municipal grant, of the *droits des pauvres*, the *secours d'hospice*, of donations or legacies to the poor, etc., these funds being apportioned among the different bureaus in proportion to the demands upon them. The bureaus are also linked with headquarters in various other ways—by the inspectors of the Director, by the accounts to be rendered, supplies of all sorts to be received from headquarters, etc[270].

Hospitals and asylums, unlike the bureau de bienfaisance, have no autonomy; their financial fusion is complete and the budget of expenses is made out and funds are furnished wholly by the central authorities. The functions of the regular *commission hospitalaire* are absorbed by the Director, who has a responsible representative in charge of each of the hospitals[271].

---

nicipal service, while indoor relief was supervised by a special council, but the former arrangement was soon resumed.

In 1880 a committee was appointed to study the organization of outdoor relief, but the municipal council disliked the solution proposed, and wanted to see out-relief completely laicized and centralized, with a single central depot and dependent dispensaries. Nothing, however, was done until 1886, when the decree of August 12, already referred to (p. 102), gave their first complete organization to the bureaus of Paris. The new law favors autonomy and simplicity. Ravarin, *loc. cit.*, pp. 361-2, 371.

[269] There is one bureau for each of the twenty arrondissements. The administration of Paris is at first sight rendered obscure by its confusing nomenclature. The whole city forms a single commune, but is divided into twenty (formerly twelve) districts, unfortunately known as "arrondissements"—the term commonly employed for the groups of cantons (themselves groups of communes) which go to make up a department. The municipal officer of the Parisian arrondissement is moreover called a maire, the name commonly appropriated to the chief official of a commune, while it is the prefect of the Seine, who exercises most of the functions of mayor of Paris.

[270] Cf. Ravarin, "L'Assistance Communal en France," pp. 368, 371, 376.

[271] Paris has twenty-one hospitals, thirteen general, eight for special classes of patients. The general hospitals are the Hotel Dieu, Notre-Dame-de-Pitié, Charité, Saint-Antoine, Necker, Cochin, Beaujon, Lariboisiere, Tenon, Laennec, Bichat, Andral, Broussais. The special hospitals are Saint-Louis, Midi, Lourcine, Enfants Malades, Trousseau, Maison d'Accouchement, Clinique d'Accouchement, Maison Municipale de Santé. Paris has beside three hospitals outside the city for scrofulous children, Berck-sur-Mer, Forge and La Roche-

There is also a bureau central des hopitaux which was originally a dispensary, the only place where consultations were offered by the public assistance and the only door of admission to the hospitals. But admission is now obtained in three ways, viz.: "d'urgence," on order of a physician at one of the free consultations now given daily in the hospitals, or through the *bureau central*, which is retained mainly as a coordinating agency and is kept informed of the number of beds available in each hospital[272].

Any one falling sick in the department of the Seine is admissible to the Paris hospitals in case there is room, but the overcrowding is great. The policy of devoting a considerable part of the funds to medical out-relief, or *secours d' hospices*, is followed[273]. To decide on admission to the *hospices*[274] a "special commission" is constituted. The possession of a "settlement" in Paris is the first requisite, but the different asylums have beside special rules[275].

The consolidation of assistance at Paris makes possible a wholesale provision for the wants of patients, attendants, offices, etc. A central bakery, installed in the Hotel Scipion, which made part of the Hôpital Général in the time of Louis XIV, was started in 1849. A model flour mill, using a process invented by M. Mége-Mouriès, to preserve the nutritious parts of the grain,was afterwards added. In 1868 a central store (*magasin central*) was instituted for the purchase and storage of articles used in the various branches of the public service, especially drygoods and household utensils. The old women from the neighboring asylum of La Salpétrière are employed there for a few cents a day in looking over bed-linen, making lint and bandages, mending, etc. There, too, are cut out and made all the dresses for the *enfants assistés* and for the patients and attendants in the hospitals

Guyon.

[272] Ravarin, "L'Assistance Communal en France,"p. 367 sq.

[273] Ravarin, "L'Assistance Communal en France," p. 370-1.

[274] The asylums and *maisons de retraite* of Paris are thirteen in number, and had in 1888 about 11,000 inmates. Few of these are in the city proper.

[275] For instance, at Sainte Périne at Auteuil, an institution fitted up with comparative luxury and intended for persons of a higher class, a minimum age of sixty and an income of 950 francs a year are required.

and asylums, all of which classes have a more or less uniform dress.

Beside the central store, bakery and mill, a special pharmacy, butchery, market agency and wine cellar have been found necessary[276].

Beside the charge of the branches of public assistance which are properly communal, the Director of the Public Assistance of Paris has also the care of the *enfants assistés*[277], which belongs regularly to the departmental authorities. The funds, indeed, are granted by the department, but they are administered by the Parisian Assistance. The care of the insane[278], on the other hand, remains in the usual hands[279].

Unions of Communes.—

Of all the complaints made against French assistance none is more general or earnest than that which charges it with breaking down in the country commune. To undertake to require every commune to support a bureau de bienfaisance, as has been often suggested, would be either to subject it to expenses it could not properly meet, or else to create a merely formal board with no funds with which to proceed, though even in the latter case this might have its use as a nucleus for donations. What is true of the bureau de bienfaisance is *a fortiori* true of the hospital and hospice; the smaller commune is too small a body to support a separate charitable organization[280]. Efforts have been made to raise the canton into a political entity intermediate between the commune and the department, but with no great success. It had either too much or too little importance, it corresponded to an artificially bounded district, it was an organization imposed from above,

---

[276]For a lively account of these *établissments généraux* see Maxime du Camp, "Paris, Ses Organes, Ses Fonctions et Sa Vie," IV, 109.

[277]See p. 127, p. 136, note 2

[278]See p. 122.

[279]Ravarin, "L'Assistance Communal en France,"p. 376.

[280]17,090 have less than 500 inhabitants, 4,328 less than 200. See fascicule 15, p. 4, of the Conseil Superieur de L'Assistance Publique. An interesting article on *L'Assistance Rurale et le Groupement de communes*, by M. E. Cheyson, appeared in the *Réforme Sociale*, September 16, and October 1, 1886.

not called into existence by actual local needs. The law of March 12, 1890, on the communal union, or *syndicat des communes*[281] seems on the contrary to fit the situation admirably. It permits the union of communes, whether or not of the same canton, for an object of intercommunal utility, defined by the decree constituting the union. Thus constituted it enjoys the *personnalité civile* which confers the right to hold property, etc. The union is administered by a committee composed of members chosen from the municipal councils of the communes represented, with, perhaps, a member or so to represent a benefactor, in case it has received private endowments. When a *syndicat* is formed for purposes of relief it has the important privilege of putting the management of indoor and outdoor relief under the management of one board, a consolidation often called for but hitherto inadmissible[282]. A commune acts with entire liberty in helping form or joining a *syndicat*, but once a member it is bound to pay its share of the authorized expenses. This form of union seems so practical, so elastic, and at the same time so firm, that it is to be hoped that it will be widely adopted and turned to account for many purposes, such as medical assistance, hospital and asylum facilities, and outdoor relief, as well as for many purposes outside of public assistance.

The Role of the Department.

The foregoing account of assistance in the commune—and especially of its prime organ the bureau de bienfaisance—shows both the strength and the weakness of this localized organization. The smaller community is the best judge of the needs and deserts of its members and the least likely to be led into extravagance; at the same time it may neglect, either from the want of means or from indifference, the most urgent and legitimate demands upon its charity, and this neglect

---

[281] Cf. Block, "Dictionnaire de l'Administration Française," article "Organization Communale," § 655 sq. See also *Conseil Supérieur de l'Assistance Publique*, No. 15.

[282] The *regime* of Paris is exceptional.

might be not only cruel to the individual but dangerous to society. The functions of the department and of the state are therefore of two sorts—supplementary and supervisory; it is especially the central power that undertakes the work of supervision, and the department that is charged with the mission of supplementing the deficiencies of communal assistance.

Supplementary Aid.—

The deficiencies of communal assistance are due to three causes—(1) to the great inequalities in the burdens thrown upon the different communes, and in their power of meeting these burdens; (2) to the rules as to settlement and admission into asylums which leave certain classes quite unprovided for, and (3) to the necessary inability of so small a unit as the commune to provide for certain needs, occurring comparatively rarely, but imperative when they do occur, and for which a departmental organization is obviously both more economical and more efficacious.

The first two classes of wants are chiefly provided for by appropriations granted by the state, and especially, as has been said, by the department. The conseil general, or council of the department, which is charged with the delicate task of assigning to the different arrondissements their respective shares of the departmental burden of taxation, is necessarily well informed as to local needs and resources, and is well fitted to do what can be done toward equalizing situations by a wise distribution of the grants from the state as well as of those from the department. There is, however, great diversity among the departments both in the amounts and in the objects of their appropriations. One of the commonest and most important goes to provide hospital treatment for the sick and incurable poor of country communes; large sums are also devoted to out-relief, especially for the sick, thus lightening the burdens of the poorer bureaus. Grants in favor of private charities, of benefit societies, of *ateliers de charité*, or to provide bourses in institutions for the blind, deaf-mutes or orphans are common. A certain sum is usually put at the disposal of the prefect under the title of "*secours en cas d'extrême misère*" to be used at his discretion. Such are some of the chief charitable "credits"[283] in the departmental budget outside those parts of public assistance which are the direct charges of the department[284].

Dépôts de Mendicité.—

The oldest charge laid upon the department is the care of the *dépôts de mendicité*, which were intended by Napoleon to be workhouses for persons convicted of beggary[285], but which have since become, to a large extent, departmental asylums for the old and feeble, especially for those unable to gain admittance to communal asylums. Though according to the Penal Code[286], begging in any locality provided with a public institution intended to obviate beggary and also habitual begging by an able-bodied person are forbidden under penal-

---

[283]Grants are also commonly made for travelling expenses in cases of need (see under "Secours de route" in Block's "Dictionnaire de l'Administration Française,"), for district doctors (*médecins cantonaux*), for the surveillance of children at nurse, and in case of local dearth or accidents.

[284]Cf. Block, "Dictionnaire de l'Administration Française," article "Assistance Publique," 14; also *ibid.*, article "Département," 93 sq.

[285] *Vide supra*, pp. 73, 74.

[286]Code Pénal, livre III, titre 1.

"274. Toute personne qui aura été trouvée mendiant dans un lieu pour lequel il existera un établissement public organisé afin d'obvier à la mendicité sera punie de trois à six mois d'emprisonnement, et sera, après l'expiration de sa peine, conduite au dépôt de mendicité." —*Pén.* 9, 40 *et s.*, 282.

"275. Dans les lieux. où il n'existe point encore de tels établissements, les mendiants d'habitude valides seront punis d'un mois à trois mois d'emprisonnement."

"S'ils ont été arrêté hors du canton de leur résidence, ils seront punis d'un emprisonnment de six mois à deux ans"—*Pén.* 9, 40 *et s.*

"276. Tous mendiants, même invalides, qui auront usé de menaces, ou seront entrés, sans permission du propriétaire ou des personnes de sa maison, soit dans une habitation, soit dans un enclos en dépendant,"

"Ou qui feindront des plaies ou infirmités,"

"Ou qui mendieront en réunion, à moins que ce ne soit le mari et la femme, le perè ou la mère et leurs jeunes enfants, l'aveugle et son conducteur,"

"Seront punis d'un emprisonnement de six mois à deux ans."— *Pén.* 9, 40 *et s.* 278.

"282. Les mendiants qui auront été condamnés aux peines portées par les articles précédents seront renvoyés, apres l'expiration de leur peine, sous la surveillance de la haute police pour cinq ans au moins et dix ans au plus."—*Pén.* 271, 463.

ties, in practice the saving clauses are liberally interpreted. In 1866 there were twenty-eight *dépôts de mendicité*[287] serving fifty-one departments (one dépôt is sometimes common to as many as eight departments), and of their 5,389 inmates only 1,237 were of the class for which they were intended, and even these did little work. Moreover, although the rule is that such persons shall be kept until they have learned to earn their living, and for a year at least, they are, in practice, held for a few weeks or months only, the funds being absorbed by the other inmates[288]. Like the hospitals, the *dépôts de mendicité* sometimes allow the communes to have their poor admitted for a certain price. This may be as little as twelve or sixteen cents a day in the dépôts, and they are then a valuable resource to the neighboring communes.

Medical Assistance.—

Though medical assistance, as a form of outrelief, is within the scope of the communal bureaux de bienfaisance, and is, on the whole, well organized in the cities, where hospitals and asylums cooperate with the bureaus, and where doctors are abundant, it is very deficient in the rural parts of France. Where medical assistance has been established in the country it is organized by departments. The question of how best to provide *"la médecine gratuite"* has been debated ever since 1810, when the first experiment was made in Alsace[289]. Three

---

[287]There are perhaps seven others which have the same name though they do not really belong in the same category.

[288]See the nineteenth "fascicule" of the *Conseil Supérieur de l'Assistance Publique*, and the chapters in regard to *dépôts de mendicité* in the works on assistance in the rural communes by Emile Chevallier, Hubert-Valleroux, and Saunois de Chevert. See also Block,"Dictionnaire de l'Administration Française," article "Mendiant."

[289]See "Nouveau Dictionnaire de l'Economie Politique," article "Médecine Gratuite," by Emile Chevallier. See also Block, "Dictionnaire de l'Administration Française," art. "Médecin Cantonal." The *Conseil Supérieur de l'Assistance Publique* devotes three of its fascicules (Nos. 9, 22 and 26), to the question of medical assistance in the country. The subject is also interestingly discussed, though with considerable repetition, in the memoirson rural assistance, by M.M. Lallemand, Hubert-Valleroux, Chevallier and Saunois de Chevert, before referred to.

systems have been advocated, and each has proved successful in some localities and unsuccessful in others.

The simplest plan is known as the cantonal system, because the prefect appoints one doctor for each canton. A list of the poor is drawn up each year by the bureau de bienfaisance, if there is one, if not by a commission, and is submitted to the approbation of the municipal council. The doctor is bound to treat any of these poor on the request of the maire or of the bureau, or, in urgent cases, of the poor themselves. Each commune has an outfit of medical necessaries, which are lent on the doctor's authorization. The objections to this system are that it leaves no liberty to the patient or the doctor, who has often too large a number of patients to attend to. According to the plan known as the *Landais*, on the other hand, the patient can call on any doctor that will accept a certain rate of payment.

In 1887 a system of "medecine gratuite" had been organized in forty-four departments, providing for 12,701 out of 18,518 communes and costing yearly 1,500,000 francs. One great difficulty in the way is the scarcity of doctors outside the cities. In certain departments there is only one doctor for eight or ten thousand inhabitants. Another difficulty is the indifference of many local and general councils, for it is on their votes of supplies that the service depends almost wholly for support. This indifference there is no means of overcoming, even in departments where the service is organized, for any commune which chooses can refuse to join in the scheme.

Care of the Insane.—

Another matter which is in the charge of the department has been already spoken of, namely the care of the insane poor. The chief point of interest here is the curious anomaly by which the expense, or rather part of it, is made obligatory for the commune, but not so for the department. Practically no department would think of refusing the necessary funds. Each department then has an asylum of its own (or one with which it has made a contract), where all dangerous lunatics, whose admission into a private establishment has not been secured by their families, are received on order of the prefect. The harmless insane are also received, subject to conditions decided on by the general council. If the patient and his family are unable to pay, the expenses are divided between the commune and the department in certain proportions, but if the patient has no settlement in any commune, for instance if he is a vagrant and his birthplace is unknown, the department bears the whole burden[290].

"Enfants du Premier Age."—

It remains to speak of the chief charitable functions of the department; those, namely, with which it is charged toward children. In ordinary cases, the child, like the adult, receives help, if help is necessary, from the bureau de bienfaisance or hospice of its commune, if there is one established. But certain classes of children are the objects of special legislation and come under the care of the departmental authorities. These classes are the so-called "enfants du premier âge," "enfants assistés" and "enfants moralement abandonnés."

The question of the proper provision for children in either physical or moral need, has received especial attention in France. In every country it is a social problem of the most vital interest to its future. No other field of philanthropic effort begins to give such promise of fruitful results, and none is, at the same time, more complicated with far reaching issues. But in France its importance is especially emphasized by several peculiarities of the national situation. The large proportion of illegitimate children, the laws in regard to them, the slow rate of growth of population, which has become a subject of general concern, the widespread custom of putting children out to

---

[290] *Vide supra* p. 93.

Block, "Dictionnaire de l'Administration Française," article "Aliénés," § 119 sq.

For a comparison of French and English administration of insane asylums, see Leroy Beaulieu, "L'Administration Locale en France et en Angleterre," p. 252 sq.

nurse—all call attention to the subject.

It is the last mentioned fact and the terrible mortality which was found to exist among the children at nurse that led to the law of December 23, 1877[291], in regard to young infants, "enfants du premier âge." Legislation on the subject is not a new thing. It even goes back as far as 1350, in which year regulations as to the "recommandaresses," or intermediaries between the parents and the nurses, were enacted. In the seventeenth and eighteenth centuries[292] the business was organized at Paris with considerable system. Four bureaus, with careful registers open to public inspection, supplied parents and nurses with a means of reaching one another and with a mutual guarantee. The nurse was required to have a certificate from the curate of her parish and endeavors were made to insure her payment by the parents.

In 1769 a single official bureau[293] was established, which undertook to serve as a means of communication between the parents and the foster mother. Inspectors, residing in their districts, were appointed to visit and report on the children at nurse. The chief difficulty was with so-called *meneurs* and *meneuses*, who carried the children back and forth, and whose dishonesty and cruelty were the cause of constant scandals. Such were the efforts made during the last century at Paris, and to some extent at least in other important cities, to prevent the evils attendant on placing children at nurse without proper supervision.

In this century no special heed was paid to the subject until 1858, when Dr. Bertillon called the attention of the Academy of Medicine to the terrible death rate among children at nurse. Dr. Monot, in 1865, found it as high as 70 per cent. among babies of a year or less

---

[291] Commonly known as the "loi Roussel," from the name of the principal author, Dr. Théophile Roussel.

[292] Lallemand, "Histoire des Enfants Abandonnés et Délaissés," p. 223 sq.

[293] Lallemand, *loc. cit.*, 225 sq. This bureau advanced the payment to the nurse subject to reimbursement from the parents, but it was so common for parents to fail to pay and to be sent to prison in consequence that special societies were formed to liberate them by paying the missing *mois de nourrice.*
Ibid, p. 227.

in the Morvan, a region devoted to this special business, whereas 10 per cent. is perhaps a not abnormal rate, and the rate even falls as low as 5 per cent. in regions where it is the custom for mothers to nurse their children. Dr. Roussel, in a famous report read to the National Assembly in 1874, confirmed these facts, and before the end of the year the "loi Roussel" was passed[294]. According to this law[295] every child under two years old put out to nurse, or sent away from home to be taken care of for money, is under the surveillance of the public authorities (Art. I). So are also the nurse, the "bureau de placement," and all intermediaries (Art. VI.) The prefect (at Paris the prefect of police), aided by a departmental committee, has charge of this surveillance, which is exercised chiefly by means of the "inspecteur des enfants assistés"[296] of the department, a state officer who collates the reports, etc., and who practically directs the whole service. Local commissions (in which two *mères de famille* must be included and where the medical inspector has a consulting voice), are instituted by the prefect where they are judged needful. The most careful registration is required; both parents and nurse must declare each child at the mairie and the nurse must have a certificate that she is a proper person for the charge[297]. There are various medical

---

[294] "Nouveau Dictionnaire d'Economie Politique," art. "Enfance," I, 815.

[295] Or rather, according to the law as supplemented by the administrative regulations of 1877.

[296] Lallemand, "Histoire des Enfants Abandonnés et Délaissés," p. 333 sq. See also Block, "Dictionnaire de l'Administration Française," article, "Enfants du Premier Age."

[297] In fact two certificates are required. The first, signed by the maire, gives the name, age, residence/profession, place of birth and état civil of the nurse, the name and profession of her husband, the age of her last child and whether it is living. It states whether the husband has given his consent to her taking a child to nurse, whether the woman's house is wholesome and neat, what are her character and means of livelihood, and whether she has a cradle and a fender. She may also be asked for information as to former nurslings. The second certificate, given by the medical inspector, or at least by a physician or health officer, and countersigned by the maire, attests the nurse's good physical condition. She is provided also with a *carnet* or pass book, in which are written the name, age, etc., of the child, the name and address of its parents, and the inventory of its *layette*. In this book are recorded the "declarations" made by the nurse, in accordance with law, (of the arrival or removal of her charge, change of residence, etc.), the visits paid by the medical inspector, and by members of the local commission if there is one, and their observations, and the dates of wages received. This pass book contains also the provisions of the penal code

and other requirements, such as that nurse and child must be vaccinated. The inspecting doctors visit the children once a month or oftener and report on their condition. The most deserving nurses receive prizes[298].

The expense of this service, which is considerable, involving as it does an immense amount of book-keeping, is borne half by the state, half by the department. But the departments not being obliged to contribute, the whole system falls to the ground where they refuse their cooperation. In 1888 four departments made no provision for the service and others provided only inadequately. Nevertheless the effect on infant mortality is perceptible. From 1868 to 1872, out of 100 children born, 18.44 died in their first year, in 1883 only 16.55[299]. In one department (Seine Inférieur) the mortality of the children coming under the surveillance of the *loi Roussel* was only 7.76, only a half or a third of that of children brought up at home. The law is moreover constantly gaining ground.

The efficacy of the law depends, of course, on the corps of inspectors, which is not as yet sufficiently numerous. Where "la médicine gratuite" is organized the question of medical inspection presents no difficulty.

---

concerning nurses and—a detail worth noting—a set of hygienic rules for the care of infants, carefully drawn up by the Academy of Medicine. With the aid of the explanations and corroborations of the visiting doctors and of the ambition wakened by the offer of rewards to the best nurses, these simple rules are capable of producing a revolution in the treatment of babies, which often, especially in country districts, suffer more from ignorance and traditional stupidity than from neglect.

[298] I witnessed an interesting scene at the yearly meeting of M. Bonjean's *Société Général de Protection pour l'Enfance Abandonné ou Coupable*, when prizes were given to nurses. One hundred francs were given to one peasant woman who, beside ten children of her own brought up at the breast, had had the care of twenty-two nurslings, fourteen of whom were brought up at the breast. She had adopted one. There were other cases nearly as remarkable.

[299] Part, at least, of the credit of these figures is due to the numerous private societies which have been organized in France, since 1865, for the "protection de l'enfance." See Lallemand, *loc. cit.*, p. 341 sq.

Enfants Assistés.—

Beside the children boarded out or at nurse whose unprotected position requires such oversight as the *loi Roussel* undertakes to provide, there are those commonly classed together as *enfants assistés* for whom complete provision must be made, and who become, for the most part, public wards.

The categories of *enfants assistés* are four—

I. Foundlings[300].

II. Abandoned children[301].

III. Destitute orphans[302].

IV. *Enfants secourus*, so called, children not adopted by the administration, whose mothers are given help on condition of their keeping instead of abandoning their babies. No child can become an enfant assiste after the age of twelve[303], but once admitted it remains under the care of the administration until majority, that is until twenty-one. In regard to this whole class of cases, or rather in regard to the deserted children who probably form its bulk, a terrible dilemma faces the legislator. How meet their needs generously without demoralizing society? How refuse free access to public adoption without increasing the already heavy number of secret crimes and infanticides? Charles

---

[300]Les *enfants trouvés* sont ceux qui, nés de pères et mères inconnus, ont été trouvés exposés dans un lieu quelconque ou portés dans les hospices destinés it les recevoir. [Decree of January 19,1811, art. 2.] Block, "Dictionnaire de l'Administration Française," article "Enfants Assistés."

[301]Les *enfants abandonnés* sont ceux qui, nés de pères et mères connus et d'abord élevés par eux ou par autres personnes à leur décharge, en ont été delaissés sans que l'on puisse recourir à eux. [Decree January 19, 1811, art. 5.] Sont assimilés aux enfants abandonnés: 1° les enfants des détenus, prévenus, accusés ou condamnés, indigents, à moins que le père ou la mère ne soit en liberté; 2° les enfants des indigents traités ou admis dans un établissement hospitalier, jusqu' à la sortie du père ou de la mère.

Ne peuvent être considerés comme abandonnés les enfants auxquels restent, à défaut de père et de mère, des ascendants tenus par la loi à leur fournir des aliments [*Code civil, art.* 205, §1,] a moins que ceux-ci ne soient dans l'impossibilité de remplir cette obligation. [*Conseil d'Etat,* 13 août 1861]

[302]Les *orphelins* sont ceux qui, n'ayant plus ni père ni mère, n'ont aucun moyen d'existence. [Decree 1811, art. 6.] Block,"Dictionnaire de l'Administration Française," article "Enfants Assistés."

[303]This limitation is prescribed by a circular of February 8, 1823. Children over twelve were considered capable of self-support. See "Les Services Publics de Protection de L'Enfance," by Loys Brueyre, p. 29.

VII already felt the difficulty in regard to admitting illegitimate children to the asylum of the Saint Esprit, and resolved the question by excluding them[304]. At the same time infanticide, and even an attempt to conceal pregnancy, was pitilessly punished, sometimes at the stake[305].

Saint Vincent de Paul and his disciples went to the other extreme, and the number of children abandoned to public charity enormously increased[306]. The Constituent Assembly expressly discharged the *seigneurs justiciers* from their old obligation to maintain the foundlings of their jurisdiction, and assumed their education as a national debt. The law of 1793, already referred to, undertook to realize this position, and also to emphasize the revolt against the conventions of the past by smoothing the path of the *fille mère* and freely permitting abandonment. Nothing, however, was accomplished[307].

With imperial reorganization, however, a permanent arrangement was at least begun. The decree of January 19, 1811[308], though very incomplete and requiring to be supplemented by administrative regulations, and though it has been largely modified by subsequent legislation, is still the *loi organique* on the subject. It embodies the revolutionary conception of a responsibility falling primarily upon the state, and the desire to encourage population[309] and to remove all temptation to infanticide and abortion by making abandonment free. One asylum (*hospice dépositaire* or *hospice designé*), each furnished with a tour[310], was to be provided in each arrondissement.

---

[304] *Vide supra*, p. 52, note (1).

[305] Lallemand, "Histoire des Enfants Abandonnés et Délaissés," p. 105 sq.

[306] 3 *Vide supra*, p. 54, sq.

[307] See Lallemand, "Histoire des Enfants Abandonnés et Délaissés," pp. 250-261, for the somewhat numerous decrees of the revolutionary bodies in regard to foundlings and orphans.

[308] Cf. Lallemand, "Histoire des Enfants Abandonnés et Délaissés," pp. 266-267; Ravarin, "L'Assistance Communal en France," p. 272.

[309] The authors of the decree stipulated that "à l'age de douze ans, les enfants mâles, en état de servir, seraient mis à la disposition du ministre de la marine." Ravarin, *loc. eit.*

[310] A *tour* is a mechanical device (said to be of Italian origin) to enable a person to deposit a child in an asylum without being recognized. An opening, usually on an unfrequented street, gave access to a receptacle, just large enough to hold a baby, which turned on a pivot so as to bring the child within the house.

This system naturally increased the number of children deserted by their parents, and the mortality in the asylums was fearful. The financial burden also was excessively heavy[311]. According to the first plan the state paid 4,000,000 francs and the hospices bore the rest of the expense, but modifications were introduced in the laws of 1837 and 1888, and by 1869, when the existing arrangement was instituted, the state had shifted most of the burden on to the department, and remained responsible only for one-fifth part of the so-called "internal expenses," and the expenses of inspection and surveillance. Accordingly the system of tours was attacked from two points of view. Economists and thinkers, like J. B. Say and De Gérando, accused it of being a cause of social evil[312], while the government, sometimes rather unconstitutionally, did its best to restrict and hamper admittance for financial reasons. In 1860 an inquiry was made, and it was found that the number of *tours*, which had been constantly diminishing, was only twenty-five, and it was decided to abolish them[313].

Since then there has been a marked difference between the practice at Paris and in the provinces. In the latter, the person abandoning a child (it is usually either the mother or *sage-femme*), is obliged to make herself known, to answer certain questions and to produce certain papers—the *acte de naissance*, etc.[314] At Paris admission is free (" à bureau ouvert") and secrecy is respected if it is strongly

---

A bell was rung at the same time to warn the person on duty inside to receive the child.

[311] Cf. a careful and interesting article on "Pauperism in France," in *The Foreign Quarterly Review*, of March, 1835 (Vol. 15). The number of foundlings in France was 69,000 in 1809; 84,500 in 1815; 102,100 in 1820; 119,900 in 1825; 125,000 in 1830. The mortality during the first year of life in the Paris asylum for children had fallen from 80 per cent., to a little over 70 per cent., against an average in France of a little over 40 per cent. The expense had risen in 1835 to 11,500,000 francs. From 1790 to 1800 the number of foundlings in the asylums more than doubled (according to Chaptal, Minister of the Interior), being in that latter year 63,000. See Lallemand, "Histoire des Enfants Abandonnés et Délaissés,"p. 271.

[312] Lamartine, however, was a warm partisan of the *tour*, which he called "an ingenious invention of Christian charity, which has hands to receive, but no eyes to see, nor mouth to reveal." "Nouveau Dictionnaire de l'Economie Politique," article "Enfance (Protection and Assistance de l')," p. 820.

[313] Lallemand, "Histoire des Enfants Abandonnés et Délaissés," p. 273 sq.

[314] Block, "Dictionnaire de l'Administration Française," article "Enfants Assistés." 12 sq.

desired[315]. This and other causes lead to the burdening of the capital with children that should properly be at the charge of the provinces.

Since their abolition many defenders of the old *tours* have appeared and the subject has given rise to endless argument. It is said that the number of infanticides has doubled within the last fifty years, and Dr. Bertillon asserts that, beside the 205 infanticides judicially recognized, there are 1,500 cases of infanticide among the alleged stillborn, and 1,400 babies purposely starved, in all 3,100.[316] These are horrid figures, but is impossible to say how much of the increase is due, not to a real growth of crime, but to increased medical knowledge, and it is impossible to estimate what part the disappearance of tours has played in the matter. It is probable that with the French people the loss of infant life and the perpetration of occasional crimes would weigh far more heavily than with an Anglo-Saxon community, when put in a balance with a lowering of the moral tone and an increase of vicious and irregular living.

With the disappearance of *tours* it came to be common to give temporary help to a "fille-mère" who would consent to keep her child. This sort of assistance, which M. Gasparin had recommended as early

---

[315]Any woman wishing to abandon her child in the department of the Seine, can either carry it to the asylum in the Rue Denfert Rochereau, or if that is too far, simply to the *commissaire de police* of the quarter. The *bulletin de naissance*, which is important to the child in after life as establishing his *état civil*, is the only paper required, and even this may be dispensed with, the mother being allowed "if she has a grave fault to hide" to declare the child "born of unknown parents." The intervention of the commissaire de police is necessary only when the mother herself does not appear. This is the system known as admission "à bureau ouvert," and has succeeded in making "exposition" (*i. e.*, deserting a child without putting it in someone's care, a punishable offense) very rare. Only fifty or so such cases occur in Paris in a year. The number of children abandoned by their parents is about 3,200 a year, which does not seem a large number in comparison with 7,200 in 1772, when Paris was only a sixth as large. This is, according to M. Brueyre (former *chef de la division des enfants assistes de la Seine*) from whom this account is taken, due to the strict rules which refuse to the mother all knowledge of where her child is sent and of everything concerning it, except that once in three months she may, if she inquire, be told whether it is alive or dead. She can, however, recover the child at any time if she can pay its back expenses, and if it be judged to be to the child's advantage. For a most vivid description of an abandonment see Maxime DuCamp's "Paris, Ses Organes, Ses Fonctions et sa Vie," IV, 275.

[316]"Nouveau Dictionnaire de l'Economie Politique," art., "Enfance, (Protection et Assistance de l')," p. 818.

as 1837, was legally instituted by the law of 1869[317]. The difference of opinion as to the merits of this plan has been great. On the one hand it has been urged that the influence of this outrelief is moral, forcing the woman to acknowledge her child, to work for it and suffer for it (for the help given is small), and that the contact with the visitors who keep run of her case is another advantage. On the other hand it has been claimed that such a system makes directly for immorality, exempting the unworthy mother from the always painful separation from her child, and making a most harmful discrimination between the honest and dishonest woman[318]. To meet this latter criticism the name of this mode of assistance has been changed to "temporary help to newborn children," or "relief to prevent desertion." It remains, however, the fact that a married mother cannot receive this help at the hands of the department, but must depend, however great her need, on the commune, that is, commonly, on the scanty and pre-carious succor of the bureau de bienfaisance, or on private charity. Most departments, to do away with this shameful distinction, now vote appropriations for "children not assisted by legal charity." Some, however, still refuse to do so. The number of "*enfants temporairement secourus*" amounted in 1887 to about one-third of all the *enfants assistés*[319]. Though the question of outrelief to mothers is an interesting one, the consideration of the other and larger part of the *enfants assistés*, whose guardianship the public authority assumes, involves still more interesting and important subjects. First is the question of how best to provide for children left, for any reason, homeless. The plan earnestly advocated by the foremost seekers after social amelioration in England and America is that of placing-out in country families, and to the usefulness and success of this method France can bring testimony drawn from a long and full experience[320].

---

[317]Lallemand, "Histoire des Enfants Abandonnés et Délaissés," p. 321-323.

[318]For a discussion of the question see Lallemand, *loc. cit.* pp. 688- 701. See also "Nouveau Dictionnaire de l'Economie Politique" *loc. cit.*

[319]See Hubert-Valleroux, "La Charité avant et depuis 1789 dans les Campagnes de France," p. 162.

[320]*Vide supra*, p. 55, sq., for a brief account of boarding out before the revolution.

The methods of admission have been already discussed. Once admitted a child is "matriculated," i. e., entered on the books of the department, which are to record every detail of its life from that time until its twelfth year. At the same time a medal with its number is fastened about its neck , not to be disturbed until it is seven years old. After these formalities the child is despatched as soon as may be to the country. At Paris, where the stay at the asylum is least, it averages only between twenty-four and thirty-six hours[321]. A large part of the children are infants (at Paris 50 per cent. are not more than a year old), and are provided with foster mothers[322]. The greatest pains is taken to find suitable places for the children, usually in farmers' families, where they grow up almost undistinguished from their foster brothers and sisters. A certain remuneration, the rate of which is fixed by the prefect and general council, is paid until the child is fourteen when it ceases except in the case of invalids or troublesome children, who have to be dealt with in asylums. Beside the amount agreed upon certain additional sums are given as a stimulus or reward[323], the most important of which is a sum of fifty francs given when a child has been well taken care of up to the age of twelve. At thirteen or fourteen a child is regularly apprenticed until the age of sixteen, preferably with a farmer, otherwise with a mechanic. If possible he is kept with his foster family. When an apprentice is sixteen the contract is renewed so as to give him as favorable terms, in regard to wages (if any), time of service, etc., as he may then be able

---

[321]Lallemand, "Histoire des Enfants Abandonnés et Délaissés," p. 281 sq.
The child must be taken also to the "bureau de l'etat civil" and registered. It must also be named if necessary.

[322]Unless at a physician's order, no child is brought up by hand. Nurses are selected and sent up from the country by the inspectors, or by special resident agents, both to get children and to remain as nurses to the children waiting to be taken to the country, and to those "en dépôt," whose parents are sick in a hospital. I saw a number of these women at the Paris asylum (Rue Denfert-Roche- reau), clean, bright-faced peasant women, in their fresh caps. There is also to be seen the strange and pitiful sight of the syphilitic children suckled by asses.

[323]Rewards are given, for instance, for sending the children to school and for religious instruction. By a decision of 1843 the children were given the right, now universal in France, of gratuitous elementary instruction. It is the duty of the maire to see that the *enfants assistés*, in his commune attend regularly at the primary school.

to command[324].

The guardianship of a child admitted to the ranks of the *enfants assistés* is vested in one of the directors of the "hospice" at which he was so admitted[325]. The choice of guardian is made by the directors as a whole, the others acting as *conseil de famille.* This guardianship, which continues until majority or "emancipation by marriage or otherwise," confers all the powers commonly belonging to the parents, except the right of reciprocal inheritance. It comprises the right to consent to marriage or enlistment, to manage property and to claim "correction[326]." If a proper person offers to accept the guardianship it may be conferred on him as a voluntary guardian, (*tuteur officieux.*)

Such is the nominal guardianship of the enfants assistes, but this does not represent the real situation. At the beginning of the century the guardians neglected the care of their wards after they had reached the age to be apprenticed, and the results were naturally bad. M. de Watteville, in his report of 1849, says that no one knows what becomes of three-quarters of the children after they are thirteen. Of those whose fate was known, 60 per cent. remained with the farmers who had brought them up, 20 per cent. were with mechanics, 10 per cent. were servants, 10 per cent. were back again in the asylums and could never be placed[327].

In 1869 the system of inspection, which previous to that time had

---

[324]Block, "Dictionnaire de l'Administration Française," article, "Enfants Assistés," 33-36.

[325]At Paris the Directeur de l'Assistance Publique is guardian of all the *enfants assistés* of the department. Lallemand, "Histoire des Enfants Abandonnés et Délaissés," p. 304, puts the number of his wards, between thirteen and twenty-one years of age, at 12,000. He has two assistants and forty-six agents living in the provinces. The latter are aided by 250 doctors.

[326]*Code Civil,* 375 sq. If a father has grave cause for displeasure at the conduct of a child under fifteen he can have him arrested and imprisoned for not more than one month. If the child be over fifteen he can be imprisoned only with the consent of the tribunal of the arrondissement and of the *procureur* of the republic, and but for six months or less. Lallemand, *loc. cit.* p. 297, says that public guardians but rarely have recourse to this power, and that usually in the case of children deserted when no longer very young and who have contracted habits of idleness or vice before admission. Such are commonly sent to agricultural "colonies" or to a House of the Good Shepherd.

[327]Page26. Quoted by Lallemand, "Histoire des Enfants Abandonnés et Délaissés," p. 302.

been very irregular, was reorganized. The departmental inspectors became state officers, paid by the state and appointed by the Minister of the Interior, and they have ever since tended more and more to become the real directors of the service[328]. The functions of guardian are practically usurped by them. They have instructions to see that the directors do their duty as guardians, and in case of failure of a guardian to comply with an inspector's recommendations, an inspector may even be appointed guardian by the prefect in his stead. This naturally creates a very anomalous state of things, and a centralization that is often complained of. It is even charged that the inspectors are, in some cases at least, political agents[329]. Of the real efficiency of such a corps of officers it is impossible to judge without a wide personal experience. Self-congratulatory official reports, and criticisms often spiced by party or religious bitterness, do not afford ground for any critical estimate. The service of *enfants assistés* being obligatory, the departmental inspectors are found throughout the country, and have been utilized for other duties than those originally assigned them, especially in connection with the execution of the *loi Roussel*, for which they are indispensable.

It remains to speak briefly of one or two legal points. First is the question of the *domicile de secours*, raised by the obligatory character of this assistance. The child is cared for by the department where it seeks and gains admittance as an *enfants assisté*, but the expenses, in so far as they fall on the department, are to be repaid by the department where the child has its *domicile de secours*[330]. This is (until a new one is acquired, and in any case until majority), the habitual residence of the mother at the time of the child's birth. After majority

---

[328] Cf. Lallemand, "Histoire des Enfants Abandonnés et Délaissés," pp. 301-309.

[329] For a criticism of this sort see Hubert-Valleroux, "La Charité avant et depuis 1789, dans les campagnes de France," A bias against the government seems evident throughout this work.

[330] Here the matter ends, as the communal contribution to the expenses of the department is irrespective of the number of children belonging to the commune who are being aided. It is otherwise in the case of the insane, where the commune pays only for its own insane. The commune in which the insane patient has his settlement must therefore be determined.

a new settlement is acquired by a year's residence. This arrangement has its objections, the main one being that it may break up a family, as the husband and wife and children may all have different settlements. The question is, however, only raised in case of insanity, desertion, or orphanage[331].

In regard to the financial burden of the service its incidence was carefully determined by the law of 1869. The state pays one-fifth of the "internal"[332] expenses and the expenses of inspection and surveillance. The communes pay among them not more than one-fifth of the "external" expenses, the conseil général of the department apportioning their respective shares, the payment of which is obligatory for them. The department pays the balance, by far the heaviest part. This is no longer obligatory for the department, but none would think of refusing to vote the necessary sum. The *hospice dépositaire* is subject to certain obligations—to provide for the supervision of the asylum, for the book-keeping, etc. Any asylum holding foundations in favor of *enfants assistés* is bound to surrender them to the *hospice dépositaire* of the department. Moreover the proceeds of certain police fines, amounting in 1884 to something under 300,000 francs, are dedicated to this branch of assistance[333].

Enfants Moralement Abandonnés.—

The strict, perhaps too strict, definition of the classes entitled to relief as *enfants assistés* shuts out many children who are equally in need of assistance, and public opinion awoke some thirteen years ago to an appreciation of the fact that numbers of vagabond and homeless children were living in suffering, and often in crime, outside the range of relief. Children otherwise coming within the requirements as to

---

[331] Ravarins' chapter on the *Domicile de Secours*, ("L'Assistance Communale en France," pp. 329-350), gives further details and is a full and interesting account of the French law with some consideration of that of neighboring countries.

[332] That is the expenses of children and nurses in the asylum and of the outfits (*layettes*) provided for the children.

[333] Cf. Lallemand, "Histoire des Enfants Abandonnés et Délaissés," p. 312 sq.

enfants assistés, but more than twelve; children whose parents were worse than dead, and who, through neglect or a systematic training in evil, were constantly appearing before the courts, but who were technically neither abandoned nor orphan—all these forlorn and dangerous social waifs, the number of whom in the capital alone was estimated at 10,000[334] became the subject of earnest attention. The law on the subject of young delinquents made the situation the more intolerable. A child arrested by a police officer for vagabondage, or petty theft from a store front, or for some similar offense, was detained at the prefecture of police while the parents were hunted up. If the boy or girl was of an age to be useful the search would not fail to be successful, and the child would be reclaimed by its parents, to whom, however unworthy, it had to be given back. In consequence the child would shortly appear again before the magistrate, and finally, grown older and more criminal, would have to be committed to a house of correction. This commitment to a house of correction was what happened in the first place if the parents did not claim the child. The language of the article of the penal code applicable in these cases is most curious. It is thus conceived:

"Art. 66. When the accused is under sixteen years of age, if it is decided that he acted without discernment, he shall be acquitted; but he shall be, according to the circumstances, given back to his parents or sent to a house of correction, to be there brought up and detained during such number of years as the sentence shall determine, which shall not, however, exceed the time when he shall have completed his twentieth year."

The *Societié Générale des Prisons* brought up the question of this class of neglected children in a meeting in 1878, and by 1881 the agitation thus started had resulted in the initial step of a reform[335]. The department of the Seine then instituted, by the side of the "service des enfantes assistés" a "service des *enfants moralement abandonnés*."

---

[334] Cf. Loys Brueyre, "Les Services Publics de Protection de l'Enfance," p. 30.
[335] Chiefly through the efforts of Mm. Quentin, Thulié and Brueyre.

These are, according to M. Brueyre's definition, "children under six-teen whom their parents leave, purposely or not, in an habitual state of beggary, vagrancy and prostitution[336].

Children of this class[337] are sent in from the courts before which they have been carried charged with some slight offense, or merely with having been found wandering in the streets; they are also brought in directly to the hospice by the police, who have orders to present any child known to them in their districts as in need of such care[338]; they are also, and these are the most numerous, brought in by their parents, who claim to be unable to control them.

All such children are kept for a preliminary fortnight at the *hospice dépositaire*, after which they may be definitely admitted. During this probationary period the children are carefully studied, the sick and weakly, and those whose moral corruption seems too great are eliminated[339], and the dispositions and aptitudes of the others noted. Those that are too young for apprenticeship are placed, like *enfants assistés*, in the country, where, says M. Brueyre, "they are permanently transformed into peasants[340]." The others are appren-

---

[336] See also "Rapport de M. Eousselsur la Protection del'Enfance," Vol. I, *annexe* V, p. 356-370. (*Vide infra*, p. 146.) The classes of children received as *enfants moralement abandonnés* are here given as follows. I. Children of from twelve to sixteen who would have been admitted, if they had been less than twelve, to the number of *enfants assistés.*, i. e., orphans, deserted children and children of convicts. II. Minors under sixteen who, arrested by the prefecture of police for small offenses or simply for being found straying in the city, were up to this time brought before the court (*déféré au parquet*), and in virtue of Art. 66 of the Penal Code, acquitted as having acted without discernment, and sent until majority to correctional institutions. III. Minors under sixteen, taken directly to the hospice by the prefecture of police after their arrest and the refusal of their parents to reclaim them; children pointed out to the administration by general and municipal councillors, by *maires* of Paris and of suburban communes, by bureaux de bienfaisance, *commissaires de police*, etc., as practically deserted by their parents, and whose admission these authorities demand.

[337] For the following account see Rapport Roussel, *loc. cit.*

[338] See a circular letter addressed by the prefect of police to his agents, printed in the report to the prefect of the Seine, of the service of maltreated and morally abandoned children for the year 1888, p. 12.

[339] The former are sent to some charitable institution or, if possible, admitted as *enfants assistés.*

[340] See a most interesting lecture entitled "Les Services Publics de Protection de l'Enfance," delivered by him before the Cercle Saint Simon, and to be had of Leopold Cerf, 13 rue de Médicis, Paris; price two francs. "We had feared at first," he says, "that used to the noise and excitement of Paris, with its factories and workshops, homesickness for the city might prevent their being contented

ticed either singly, or in groups, with manufacturers who are willing to take them and give them personal care. An account is opened between the administration and each child on his admission, and it is expected that by the time he is his own master he will have repaid all except general expenses, and have in the bank a small capital of from 500 to 2,000 francs or more.

Four technical schools, one for horticulture and basketwork, one for cabinetmaking, one for printing, and one, for girls, for artificial flower making, have also been founded.

As to the results of this system the figures for the first five years as given by M. Brueyre are as follows[341]:

Of 4,000 children received, 3,400 were still under the care of the administration.

Of these about 8 per cent. ran away, could not be kept, or were sent to a reform school established for the purpose[342].

The expenses were on the average 125 francs a year for each child, and the average sum in the savings bank to the credit of each was 12.50 francs. Of course, in only five years comparatively few would have reached the point where they could be expected to save. In these five years the number of children sent to houses of correction fell from 10,000 to 8,000, but at least part of the credit of this decrease must be given to the vigorous private efforts made in the same direction[343]

---

and successful in the country. Great was our surprise, great our pleasure when, after some years experience, the reports of our agents unanimously reported the success of the experiment."

[341] "Les Services Publics de Protection de l'Enfance," p. 52.

[342] The reform school established at Porquerolles was not a success and was given up.

[343] The statistics of the *service des enfants moralement abandonnés* as given in the official report of 1888 above referred to are as follows:

Present December 31, 1887 2,794 Entered during 1888 676 Total 3,470 Discharged during 1888 503 Returned to family 319 Discharged at majority 70 on marriage 1 on enlistment 2 Died 14 Transferred to class of "Enfants Assistés" 13 Escaped* 84 Remaining December 31, 1888 2,967 .

*Of these only nine were lost sight of. The others returned to their families. It must be remembered that the public assistance had at this date no legal authority over these children.

The children were placed as follows:

boys. oirm. Boarded while waiting to be apprenticed.... 568 245 Apprenticed singly 1,054 346 in groups* 237 141 In technical schools. t Villepreux, Montevrain, Alen<;on 149 — Yzeure — 93 In various establishments 12 47 Under

Meanwhile it was only at Paris that there was any public provision for the class of "morally abandoned" children, and even there the efforts made in their behalf were often neutralized by the lack of legal authority. Even the parent who had voluntarily surrendered a child[344], still retained the "puissance paternelle," and could reclaim the boy or girl when of an age to be useful. Some of the cases were heartrending, particularly those of girls surrendered against their will

---

hospital treatment at Berck and Saint Broladre 15 24 " In preservation" (that is in prison or in a reform school) 19 5 At the hospice, December 31 8 4 2, (.162 905 Of those admitted in 1888 there were: boys, 478; girls, 198; legitimate, 561; illegitimate, 115; ten years old or less, 311; ten to twelve, 151; twelve to fifteen, 170; fifteen and over, 44; sent by the parquet, 40; by the prefecture of police, 154; presented by their parents, 482.‡

*The size of these groups varied from two to forty-one, and comprised sixty-three different professions for the boy apprentices, twenty for the girls. Instances are cited of pupils arrived at majority continuing at work in the same place and getting other members of the family to join them there.

†Villepreux has twenty-six pupils, and teaches gardening and basketwork. The Ecole Alembert at Montevrain with eighty-six pupils has a school of cabinetmaking and a printing office. Alençon is for teaching printing and has thirty-eight pupils. The school at Yzeure for girls was only started during the year covered by the report. Sewing was apparently the only thing then taught outside the ordinary school branches.

‡The court or the police on the arrest of a child possibly a fit subject for this service send it directly to the headquarters of the public assistance. Though the service was instituted to protect children against unworthy parents, it has been more largely employed in taking care of children whose parents could not control them, and who either requested the administration to take charge of them or, what amounted to the same thing, refused to take them back after arrest. Children are received as young as six; with those above a certain age and apparently hopeless the law is allowed to take its course.

As regards the character of the children or their parents the statistics for those admitted in 1888 are as follows:

1.	Parents poor		337
2.	"	unworthy	71
3.	"	disappeared	75
4.	"	dead	142
5.	Children vicious		51

676

That is, even assuming all the parents who are entered as "disappeared" to have been unworthy, less than 24 per cent. were of the class specially aimed at by the law of 1889—children of vicious parents.

Of 5,619 children admitted since the establishment of the service (January 1, 1881), 22.12 per cent, were born outside the department of the Seine, and 2.66 per cent. were of foreign nationality, but of these latter more than half were from Alsace and Lorraine.

[344]Even after signing an agreement (such as is quoted by M. Boussel, *loc. cit.*) to surrender all authority "as far as law allows," the parent could reclaim the child at any time.

to an unnatural mother[345]. Already in 1880 a parliamentary committee had been appointed to study how this state of things could best be remedied, and from that time until July 24, 1889, when a law known as the "law on the protection of maltreated or morally abandoned children" was finally voted, the question was more or less before the legislature. The history of the different propositions, of which that of M. Roussel was the most far-reaching, is a complicated one[346]. Its chief incident was the voluminous report communicated to the Senate by M. Roussel, in 1882, giving the results of researches in regard to laws and institutions for child-helping in all civilized countries.

The law as finally passed is mainly occupied with legal details as to guardianship and paternal rights. A parent forfeits *de plein droit the puissance paternelle*, with its associated rights[347], on conviction for certain grave offenses[348], including crime against the child's person, complicity in a crime committed by the child, or exciting or favoring its prostitution or corruption. The same forfeiture may, at the discretion of the court, be pronounced in other cases[349], viz., on first conviction for habitually exciting minors to debauch, when a child has been sent to the house of correction as having "acted without discern-

---

[345] Such a case is among those cited by M. Roussel, *loc. cit.* Two girls were arrested, and the elder, who was sixteen, applied, with her mother's consent, to be admitted into one of the institutions for the "moralement abandonnés." The mother afterwards got the second girl admitted, and both were placed in a silk factory and there gave complete satisfaction. The mother, however, got a considerable sum of money given her through newspaper articles which she deluded journalists into publishing for her, and came to demand her daughters. In spite of the elder girl's repugnance and the known bad character of the mother they had to be given up, and were seen a few days later "vêtues avec un luxe tapageur du plus mauvais présage."

[346] For a concise account of it see a pamphlet by Léon Lallemand reprinted from the "Annuaire Français de la Société de la Legislation Comparée," 1890.

[347] The *puissance paternelle* comprises the right of fixing the residence of the child, *Code Civil*, 108; the right of consenting to marriage, 148, 151; the right of consenting to adoption, 346; the right of consenting to a "tutelle officieuse," 361; the right of direction, custody, correction, enjoyment of property and administration, 372-387, 389; the right of guardianship, of designation of a council to surviving mother, and of the appointment of a guardian, 390, 391, 397; the right of emancipation, 447; the right of agreeing to contracts of apprenticeship, decree of February 22, 1851; the right of agreeing to enlistment, law of July 27, 1872. Obligations as to maintenance are not however abrogated. For these obligations see the *Code Civil*, 205, 206, 207.

[348] Article 1.

[349] Article 2.

ment," and, even without previous conviction, against parents who by their habitual drunkenness, notorious and scandalous misconduct or ill treatment compromise either the health, safety or morality of their children.

The official interpretation of this clause, and instructions to the magistrates in regard to it, are extremely conservative. "It is important that the intervention of the courts, outside the cases where it is formally required by the law, should be undertaken only with the greatest circumspection and quite exceptionally, in cases where there could not rise the slightest doubt of its timeliness[350]."

The guardianship when not given to the mother or provided for in the usual way, is regularly to be exercised by the public assistance. It may, however, be granted to a person making application at the time of trial, or to a person with whom the public assistance has placed the child, on applying after three years.

Titre II of the law provides that when public charitable bodies, charitable societies authorized to this effect[351], or private individuals have taken the charge of minors of sixteen at the request of their parents or guardians, the *puissance paternelle* may, on the request of the parties interested, be judicially conferred on the public assistance, which may then delegate its exercise to the institution or individual who has taken charge of the child.

The next case taken up is that of children of sixteen or under taken charge of by an institution, public or private, or by an individual, *without the intervention of the parents*. In such instances notice must be given to the proper authority within three days, under pain of a fine, and the parents are then notified. If the child remains unclaimed for three months the person or institution may then be given all or part of the rights of the paternal power. If the parent subsequently presents his claim to this power he may be declared to have lost it.

---

[350] "Cireulaire addressée par M. le Garde des Sceaux, Ministre de la Justice et des Cultes, à Mm. les procureurs généraux au sujet de l'application de la loi du Juillet, 1889, sur la protection des Enfants Maltraités ou Moralement Abandonnés."

[351] Such authorization would have to be subsequent to this law, since such a contingency as the need of it could not have been foreseen.

The child confided to a society or an individual under this law is under the oversight of the state, represented by the prefect, and also of the Public Assistance represented by its agents the departmental inspectors of assisted children (in Paris by the Director of Public Assistance). The child may, if the courts deem it for his interest, be given at any subsequent time into the entire charge of the Public Assistance.

Finally, it is enacted that when a department will put *enfants morale-ment abandonnés* on the same footing as *enfants assistés* as regards expense, the state grant shall be raised to one-fifth of both the external and internal expenses for both classes, and the contribution of the communes shall be obligatory for both.

This law, though essentially a compromise measure, and far from realizing all the plans of the reformers, goes far to rectify the exaggerated respect for parental rights inherited by French law from Rome[352], and to insure to preventive philanthropy a fair field for its efforts. It is however marred by the prevalent distrust of private agencies and fondness for governmental control. It is confused in its attribution of the same power to two differents sets of agents, prefects and inspectors, and gives to the inspector the responsible position of guardian without the usual check of a conseil de *famille*[353], and without responsibility except to his official head the prefect.

---

[352] For interesting remarks on the *patria potestas*, see the beginning of Volume III of Roussel's report, and also the report on a bill for the Protection of Children, made to the Senate, December 8, 1881, by M. Cazot, Minister of Justice.

The French conception is, says M. Cazot, a compromise between the absolute right of Roman law and the Germanic idea of ward and protection. The rights and privileges of a father are laid down in Titre IX of the Civil Code. There is an obligation toward the child to support and educate him, but the failure to fulfill these obligations does not *ipso facto* deprive the father of his rights. The only case provided for by the Penal Code, (Art. 335), is the encouragement of prostitution and corruption.

[353] This is indeed a marked innovation, every guardian, except a father during the lifetime of his wife, having associated with him a *conseil de famille*. This is provided for in the case of *enfants assistés* by letting one member of the commission of an asylum hold the guardianship and the rest act as council. The only exception, and this is an important one, is in the case of the Directeur de l'Assistance Publique at Paris, who is guardian of some thousands of wards without any council. See above p. 136.

Objection[354] has also been made to the use of the title *l'Assistance Publique* as if this existed as an independent branch of the government. The fact is that it consists of nearly autonomous local institutions of various sorts supervised by a central board, known as the *Direction de l'Assistance Publique*, belonging to the department of the Minister of the Interior. Another criticism has been that the promises of state subvention, with which the law closes, commit the government to expenses of an entirely unknown amount.

With this too hasty discussion of the interesting subject of neglected children, we must leave the consideration of the functions of the department and turn to those of the central government.

The Role of the State.

The main functions of the state in regard to public assistance are the constitution and regulation of such assistance by the legislature, and the direction and surveillance of its whole administration by the Minister of the Interior and his agents, represeresenting the executive.

State Grants. —

Beside this the state bears its share, though a comparatively slight one, of the financial burden. In 1885 the figures were as follows[355]:

Total receipts for uses of public assistance— Francs. Percent. State 7,511,956 .04 Departments 29,912,459 .16 Communes (without Paris) 28,309,483 .15 Paris :23,508,198 .13 From private sources, gifts and foundations 94,879,003 .52 184.121,099 100

The only appropriations which the state is bound to supply are those required by the provisions of the law as to "assisted children," the "*loi Roussel*" and the law as to "neglected and morally abandoned

---

[354] Cf. Lallemand, in the paper mentioned above. See also p. 163.

[355] These figures are those of M. Monod. Cf. Levasseur, "La Population Française," t. Ill, p. 140.

children."

In that same year grants of something over a million were made to the "établissements nationaux de bienfaisance." These are state institutions open equally to all Frenchmen and under the direct charge of the Minister of the Interior. They are ten in number, and make rather a heterogeneous list, viz.: the blind asylum of the Quinze-Vingts, the insane asylum of Charenton, the deaf mute institutions of Paris, Chambery and Bordeaux, the "Institution des Jeunes Aveugles" at Paris, two convalescent asylums,—one for men at Vincennes, one for women at Vésinet—the asile Vacassy for victims of accidents, and, finally, the hospice of Mont Genevre for travelers crossing the Alps. Some of these institutions are very ancient; the Quinze-Vingts was founded or enlarged by St. Louis; the Alpine hospice, which in 1885 succored 4,500 travellers, dates from only a century later. Valentine Häuy, the Abbé Sicard and the Abbé de l'Epée were, with Louis XVI, the authors of the various asylums for the deaf and blind, except the Quinze-Vingts and the asile de Chambéry. The latter was a Savoyard institution, and became French with the annexation of Savoy in 1861. Others of the national asylums are very recent, the latest being the asile Vacassy.

All these institutions have funds of their own and are only partly dependent on the state grant, which often goes to found *bourses* (scholarships or free beds), at the disposition of the Minister of the Interior[356].

Besides the grants to national establishments a nearly equal sum is distributed, with the advice of the general councils of the departments, among various public and private charitable institutions. In 1885, for instance, 383,000 francs went to bureaux de bienfaisance, 43,000 to hospitals and asylums, 104,000 to private institutions. Since 1888, however, the amount thus distributed has been reduced and at the same time its employment has been restricted to exceptional cases, to institutions in particular distress for want of means, or to peculiar

---

[356]For further details in regard to these institutions, see "Conseil Supérieur de l'Assistance Publique," fasicule 10. See also Saunois de Chevert, "L'Indigence et l'Assistance dans les Campagnes depuis 1789 jusqu' à nos jours," pp. 111-125.

and accidental cases of poverty. The extreme subdivision formerly necessitated—80 francs being the average share of an institution—and the routine distribution which was the custom, made this grant almost useless previous to this reform.

Other objects for which state grants are allowed are: To aid in establishing medical assistance for rural districts; to encourage *sociétés de charité maternelle* and day nurseries (crèches), and to repay expenses incurred for persons without a settlement. Finally certain charitable funds are disposed of outside the public assistance office as *secours personels*. These are mainly in the hands of the "*direction de la sûreté publique*," and are not, I think, publicly accounted for. Certain sums are also devoted to foreign refugees and to *frais de repatriement*, i. e., to bringing home French citizens overtaken by poverty away from their commune or from their country.

Beside the appropriations thus allowed for state charity two or three million francs are supplied by special funds known as *secours spéciaux pour pertes matérielles et évènements malheureux*[357], furnished by a special *centime additionel* added to the chief direct taxes. These are distributed to the victims of disasters of various sorts, especially to those suffering from fire, floods or loss of crops or stock by blight, hail, frost or disease. A small sum, not more than two hundred francs at most. is sometimes given to a man suffering from a personal accident, or to his widow, but as as a usual thing the money goes to help remedy widespread calamities. The rate of relief is fixed each year according to the yield of the tax and the average losses to be met. At present an indemnity for five per cent. of the loss is allowed. Help is given, however, only in cases of need.

In cases of exceptionally serious trouble special temporary credits are often voted by the chambers, or by a municipal or departmental council.

The criticisms brought against this state aid in case of accidents is that it lends itself to political abuse, and that the rate is too low to

---

[357]Cf. Block, "Dictionnaire de l'Administration Française," Art. "Sinistres (Secours spéciaux en cas de)."

be a material help unless the assessment of damages is unfair[358]. It would seem too as though it would tend to discourage private insurance[359].

Besides the distribution of money, sufferers from accidents enjoy a considerable remission of taxes (dégrèvement). The remission on the two main taxes, that on real estate and that on doors and windows, cannot be considered public assistance; these taxes being essentially taxes on revenue or capital, and not due when that is destroyed. Remission of these taxes is, accordingly, granted irrespective of the means of those who have suffered from the accident. On the other hand remission of the *contribution personelle-mobilière* or of the *patentes* is accorded only in case of need. The funds to meet these degrevements are supplied by *centimes additionals* added to the four regular taxes; this addition to the *contribution personelle-mobilière* is at the rate of one centime per franc (1 per cent), to the *patentes* at the rate of 5 per cent.

Savings, Insurance and Monts de Piété.—

The patronage or the direct assistance extended by the state to agencies for promoting thrift may also be reckoned as, in a sense, a part of its public charity. But the subject is a broad one and, though interesting from several points of view, a little outside the scope of this

---

[358] Cf. Hubert-Valleroux, "La Charité avant et depuis 1789, dans les campagnes de France," p. 151 sq. "N'a ton pas vu récemment un sous-préfet (celui de Bernay) répondre aux habitants d'un village victime d'un sinistre et qui demandaient à avoir part aux fonds de secours: Ces secours (fournis par les contribuables) sont une faveur que le gouvernement accorde à ses partisans et qu'il refuse à ceux qui ont mal voté? Comme ce fonctionnaire n'a été ni déplacé ni même blâmé, il faut croire que sa réponse n'avait pas déplu au ministre, son supérieur."

[359] The prevalence of insurance against loss by fire or otherwise seems, however, to be satisfactory in France. Insurance against fire covers about four-fifths of the losses (80-85 per cent. for real property, 70-82 per cent. for personal property, 65-70 per cent. for crops in granaries, 70-80 per cent. for crops standing or in the mill, 10-30 per cent. only for woods). The loss from fire in France, omitting the department of the Seine, varies from about 45,000,000 to 60,000,000 a year. The valuations of loss through accidents, etc., presented by the minister of finance and those of the minister of commerce vary greatly however. See De Foville, "La France Economique," p. 399.

paper and only an outline of it can be attempted. The earliest provident institution established in France was a savings bank. Though the idea of such a bank had been conceived by a Frenchman as early as 1611, and though the proposal to create one had been vigorously discussed by Mirabeau and Robespierre in 1789, it was finally from England that the organization was borrowed. This was in 1818, when a *caisse d'épargne et de prévoyance de la ville de Paris* was founded by two great philanthropists, La Rochefoucauld-Liancourt and Benjamin Delessert. This bank and the numerous others which imitated it were managed by private societies and were often well endowed. They were soon, however, subjected to certain governmental regulations. The chief is that the deposits must be at once transferred to the Caisse des Dépôts et Consignations which serves interest at a rate fixed by law—since 1853 at 4 per cent[360]. This rate is a considerable burden on the treasury and a source of abuses, leading small capitalists to use the banks as an investment. In 1888 there were some 1,500 banks and branches, with more than 5,000,000 depositors and a debt of nearly 2,500,000,000 francs[361].

In 1874 an advance was made with the institution of school savings banks. By 1886 there were nearly 24,000 of these, holding almost 12,000,000 of francs belonging to about 500,000 scholars[362].

In 1881 the national or postal savings bank was organized, after the English model. Deposits of a franc or over are received at any post office, and stamps may be bought and saved to make up that amount and then deposited instead of money. In every way pains are taken to make saving simple and attractive. The funds thus collected are, like those of private savings banks, administered by the Caisse des Dépôts et Consignations, but a slightly lower rate of interest is allowed. In the first seven years of its existence the postal bank received deposits amounting to 300,000,000 francs, from more than 1,000,000

---

[360] Block, "Dictionnaire de l'Administration Française," article "Caissse des Dépôts et Consignations," §92; See also article " Caisses d'Epargne Privées."

[361] *Annuaire de l'Economie Politique et de la Statistigue*, 1891, p. 176 sq.

[362] "Nouveau Dictionnaire d'Economie Politique," article '"Epargne," p. 927. See also Saunois de Chevert, "L'Indigence et L'Assistance dans les Campagnes," p. 235-236.

persons[363].

Not so successful have been the attempts of the state to organize pension and insurance funds. In 1850 a *caisse des retraite pour la vieillesse* was created to receive small deposits toward a pension payable at the age of fifty. If the depositor chose, the pension could begin later at a somewhat higher figure or, in case of serious infirmities, earlier at a lower figure. The maximum pension was set at first at 600 francs a year. The arrangements were such as to leave a heavy balance for the government to shoulder[364], and at the same time did not prove strongly attractive to the working classes for whom the institution was meant. Out of nearly 8,000,000 payments only something over 200,000 were made directly, most being paid by large companies for the employees on their pension roll or by benefit societies. In 1886 the caisse was reorganized on a somewhat wiser basis. The process of making deposits was simplified, and the maximum pension was raised to 1,200 francs a year. Nevertheless the majority of its clientele is of the same character as before[365].

The state has also undertaken to manage a caisse of life insurance, and one of insurance against accidents occurring during agricultural or industrial labor. Both were founded in the wane of the second empire, and neither is of any great value. They are indeed very little patronized, which is fortunate for the treasury, as the arrangements of the former are such as to leave a large deficit[366], while at least half the funds destined to be paid in accident cases is drawn not from premiums but from gifts or state grants[367].

Benefit societies, or *sociétés de secours mutuels*, though private associations, stand in a peculiar relation to the state, and receive special

---

[363] "Nouveau Dictionaire D'Economie Politique," p. 926.

[364] Estimated at 72,000,000 for the perion 1875-1882.

[365] "Nouveau Dictionnaire D'Economie Politique," article "Retraites," p. 724 sq.

[366] This life insurance caisse received in 1889, 48,736 francs on individual policies, 100,101 francs from 89 *Sociétés de Secours Mutuels.* The accident *caisse* in the same year received some 1,328 subscriptions and paid one indemnity. "Annuaire de l'Économie Politique and de la Statistique," 1891, p. 67-68.

[367] See Block, "Dictionnaire de l'Administration Française," article "Assurance," §90.

privileges at its hands. Up to 1852 they were merely supervised to a greater or less degree, but according to a decree of March 26 of that year one was to be instituted by the maire and cure in any commune where the prefect and municipal council should declare one to be desirable. Official "approbation," which is easily obtainable, confers special privileges—a share of a state grant of ten million francs, a free place of meeting to be furnished by the commune, alleviation of taxes, special rates from the Caisse des Dépôts et Consignations on funds destined to go toward annuities, honorary rewards to members and many other encouragements[368].

At the beginning of this century there were forty-five *sociétés de secours mutuels* in France; from 1813 to 1840, 451 were established. The freedom of association proclaimed by the revolution of 1848 and the paternal legislation of the next years gave them a fresh start, so that in 1853 there were nearly 2,700. In 1887 there were 8,409 societies, of which 6,093 were "approved." These latter embraced over a million members, of whom be it noted, for the fact is significant, nearly 200,000 were "honorary" members, who help support but receive no benefit from the society[369].

A much more interesting instance of state encouragement of thrift, or rather of interference to prevent waste through recklessness or deception, is the governmental monopoly of pawnshops. Special monts-de-piété had been established under the old regime, but their privileges were contrary to the principles of the revolution, and the business of pawnbroking was then thrown open. The law of 16 Pluviôse, year XII (Febuary 6, 1804), however, again forbade its exercise except under governmental sanction and for the profit of the poor, and the Penal Code (1810) reiterated the prohibition.

The matter is at present mainly regulated by the provisions of the law of June 24, 1851. The monts-de-piété are corporations, instituted as "establishments of public utility," with constitutions, accordingly,

[368] Block,"Dictionnaire de l'Administration Française," Article, "Sociétés de Secours Mutuels."

[369] De Foville, "La France Economique," p. 401-402. The figures include Algerian societies.

116

approved by the Council of State. They are managed by a board presided over by the maire (in Paris by the prefect of the Seine) and a director appointed by the minister or prefect.

There are now forty-two monts-de-piété in France, of which that of Paris, with its branches, is by far the most important, doing more business than the rest all together. In 1889 the number of pawnings was in all over three million, and the sums lent nearly sixty million francs[370].

Certain monts-de-piété, largely endowed, make loans without interest, but except in these special cases it is required that the rate shall be above the legal five per cent. and it actually averages eight percent., being in some instances as high as twelve or fifteen per cent. per annum[371]: The loan is usually fourfifths of the bullion value of articles of gold and silver, two-thirds of the appraised value of other goods. Pawns are usually retained one year, when, if not renewed, they will be sold at auction. The excess of the receipt at sale over the sum loaned may be claimed by the pawner any time within three years, on presentation of the *reconnaisance* or ticket. To prevent traffic in these tickets any person requiring to realize the full value of a pawn may have it sold at the end of three months.

When the interest together with the *boni* (or the unclaimed profits of auctions) are more than enough to cover expenses and to pay interest on borrowed capital it may be funded with the object of lowering the loan rate. When, however, the rate is already as low as five per cent. the excess must, except where the mont-de-piété is especially allowed to have a lower rate, be handed over to the hospitals, or other charitable establishments. In 1891 the budget of the public assistance of Paris received 180,000 francs from this source[372].

Even at the high rate of interest prevailing it is estimated that seventy-six per cent. of the loans are made at a loss. It is the comparatively few considerable borrowers, to whom secresy and security

---

[370] *Annuaire de l'Economie Politique el de la Statistique*, p. 393.

[371] In Paris it is nine per cent., payable in twelfths. Saunois de Chevert, "L'Indigence et L'Assistance dans les Campagnes," p. 223.

[372] *Annuaire de l'Economie Politique et de la Statistique,* p. 597.

are more important than the rate of interest, who make the balance right. These facts, granting that the business management is good, show what an advantage the institution is to the small borrower, who, in dealing with an irresponsible pawnbroker doing business on his own account, would not only run a risk of being unfairly used, but, at the best, would have to pay a rate of interest such as to recoup the broker for the small borrowers' full share of the general expenses, and that on a retail scale.

The raising of money on personal property is not only a legitimate but a necessary resource to the classes whose only capital is in this form. It is by no means always an unthrifty proceeding, perhaps not even generally so, but as carried on in most cities where the regime of private pawnbroking prevails it is made to seem, and therefore tends to be, a downward step. It would seem as though it be an inestimable gain to the police as well as to the general *morale* of a great city, to have pawnshops such as congregate on back streets in American cities replaced by monts de piété like those of Paris, where the deposit of stolen goods is difficult and rare and their recovery easy, where the process of pawning is simple and proper, and though expensive, not ruinous, and above all without risk. Indeed the gain seems so obvious and so great that it is surprising that more serious study has not been given to the plan in this country[373].

Judicial Assistance. —

Another form of state charity is judicial assistance (assistance judiciaire). The need of free justice for the poor had been felt from the earliest period of the French monarchy and orders were given again

---

[373] On the subject of monts de piété the comprehensive work of M. Blaize, a former director of the mont de piété of Paris may be consulted with profit: "Des Monts-de-Piété des Banques de Prêt sur Gage en France et dans les divers pays de Europe," Pagnerre, 1856. For facts as to organization see M. Richlot's article in Block's "Dictionnaire de l'Administration Française," See also an article on the general subject in the "Nouveau Dictionnaire d'Economie Politique,"; Ravarin, "L'Assistance Communale en France," pp. 145-148; and the fascicules of the Conseil Supérieur de l'Assistance Publique bearing on the matter.

and again that it was to be provided[374], perhaps with some remembrance of the Roman law in mind. But under the old order justice was hard to come by without a heavy purse, and it was the Constituent Assembly that, by declaring justice free and suppressing the fees levied by the judges, made the need of such measures comparatively small.

After the revolution, however, both law and legal custom continued to provide help for poor suitors. By the law of January 22, 1851, "bureaus of judicial assistance" were established, by the side of the various tribunals, to examine the proofs of the poverty of those claiming judicial assistance. They might also act as boards of conciliation. The person assisted is dispensed from all the usual fees as well as from the deposit of a possible fine (*consignation d' amende*) where this is required.

In criminal, "correctional" and police cases the procedure is different. When the accused can prove his poverty the judge may, of his own motion, appoint some one to act as counsel, order witnesses called, papers produced, etc[375].

Requests for judicial assistance are on the increase[376]. They are commonest in civil cases and especially in suits for divorce or separation.

---

[374]Cf. the provisions of the capitularies quoted by Granier, "Essai de Bibliographie Charitable," p. 84. and the ordinance of Charles V, given by Monnier, "Historie de l'Assistance Publique," p. 305, note 2, as follows:

Reglement pour les Reguestes du Palais, ou Ordonnance sur l'administration de la justice, les devoirs des magistrals, ceux des avocats, des procureurs et des sergens. Paris, novembre, 1364.

Art. 6. Nous voulons et commandons estroictement que tous les advocas et procureurs frequentans et qui frequenteront le siege desdites requestes soient au conseil, pour Dieu, des povres et miserables personnes qui y plaident et plaideront; et que ad ce nosuites gens contraingnent lesdits advocaz et procureurs; et que à telles et pour telles povres et miserables personnes nosdites gens, quant les cas y escherront, facent, pour Dieu, leurs requestes et pieces, et les oyent diligemment, et les delivrent briefment.
See also Block, "Dictionnaire de l'Administration Française," article "Assistance Judiciare," § 1.

[375]See Block, "Dictionnaire de l'Administration Française," Article, "Assistance Judiciaire," law of January 22, 1851.

[376]See *Annuaire de l'Economie Politique et de la Statistique,* p. 570. The demands at the *bureaux d'arrondissement* were 35,651 in 1883, 58,250 in 1888.

Administration. —

Public assistance belongs as has been said to the department of the Minister of the Interior. This means not only that he has in his hands the management of the national institutions and the distribution of certain grants, but that directly or indirectly he may largely affect the policy of public charitable institutions throughout the country. The large amount of influence reserved to his subordinates, the prefects, as to the make up of boards of management of hospitals, asylums and bureaux de bienfaisance[377] and the control exercised over all the proceedings of these bodies has been already commented upon[378]. The minister, moreover, supervises all public charitable institutions through his "general inspectors[379]." He has also the nomination of the departmental inspectors of *enfants assistés* whose preponderance in that department of assistance has been complained of[380].

Another function of the minister is to announce and comment upon new laws, affecting his department, in circular letters to his subordinates. Any functionary, a prefect, for instance, expressly charged by a law with a certain duty does not feel at liberty to comply until he has been thus instructed by his superiors. This system makes it possible to pass laws which simply lay down the principles, leaving it to the administrative authorities to make the necessary regulations, or even to simply entrust a branch of the administration with some public service, leaving it entire latitude as to execution[381]. Ministerial instructions are accordingly circulated whenever need arises, and

---

[377] Viz. the appointment of two-thirds of their number.

[378] See p. 82sq.
It is to be noted that the French law considers all public establishments, departments, communes and asylums as minors, and charges the state or the administration with the exercise of guardianship. This *tutelle administrative* chiefly concerns the care of property, purchases, sales, contracts, litigations, etc. See Block, "Dictionnaire de l'Administration Française," article "Tutelle Administrative."

[379] There were five of these inspectors in 1889. The number of institutions is so great that a complete round of visits is said to take four years.

[380] Cf. p. 137.

[381] See Block, "Dictionnaire de l'Administration Française," article "Administration," §9, and article "Ministère," §37 sq.

not only serve to interpret and sometimes materially to modify the law[382], but add to it a considerable body of supplementary regulation binding, it is true, upon officials only, but important as a matter of fact.

In the matter of the direction of public assistance important developments have taken place within the last five years. First, by a decree of November 4, 1886, all the branches of public assistance under the charge of the Minister of the Interior, were united under a single management, to which were also afterwards confided most of the departments of puhlic hygiene previously under the charge of the Minister of Commerce[383]. The new board known as the *Direction de l'Assistance Publique* was divided into four *bureaux* or committees, having for subject matter, (1) national institutions, beggary, the insane; (2) children; (3) communal hospitals and asylums, bureaux de bienfaisance, public hygiene; (4) benefit societies, monts-de-piété.

The object of this board is well expressed in the preamble of the decree creating it.

"The most characteristic and fruitful part of this recasting will be the union of the scattered fragments of our charitable services in a single whole...... It is well to remember that the different pieces of legislation which control it have almost never been inspired by general principles, and that no thought of a whole presided at its elaboration. At a time when questions of public assistance are the order of the day and intensely interest all minds, it seems indispensable for the administration to do all in its power to be worthy of its task. The creation of a board whose special charge it is to administer charitable legislation marks a real step forward in that it makes it possible to study the question as a whole."

In 1888 there was instituted a further body known as the *Conseil Supérieur d'Assistance Publique*, composed of some sixty members, part appointed, part *ex-officio*. Like the "Direction" it is divided into four sections, though the subjects assigned to them are differently

---

[382] A marked instance is a ministerial circular of 1823 excluding from the ranks of *enfants assistés* categories not shut out by law. See Lallemand, "Histoire des Enfants Abandonnés et Délaissés," p. 274 sq; See also above, p. 128, note 4.

[383] Block, "Dictionnaire de l'Administration Française," article "Assistance Publique," §20.

121

distributed[384].

In this council the most competent authorities on matters of public charity, both practical administrators and officials, meet to discuss important questions, to prepare or criticise draughts of laws and to act as a consulting committee for the executive. Thirty or more "fascicules" containing the proceedings of various sessions, reports, bills, statistics, etc., have been issued and constitute most valuable mines of information as to present conditions of public assistance and the reforms in contemplation[385].

A reorganization of public assistance is the openly expressed object of the institution of this council, and if it is effected according to the wishes of the council, it is likely to be a marked advance toward a system of obligatory charity. M. Floquet, then Minister of the

---

[384] These are—
(1) Services de l'Enfance.
(2) Secours aux indigents valides ou malades.
(3) Secours aux indigents malades ou incurables.
(4) Etablissements généraux, aliénés, monts de piété, dépôts de mendicité.
[385] The list of subjects is as follows—
1. Constitution du Conseil Supérieur de l'Assistance Publique.
2. Direction de l'Assistance publique; Inspection générale.
3. Budget de l'Assistance publique pour 1888.
4. Enfants assistés.
5. Enfants protégés.
6. Crêches, Sociétés de Charité Maternelle.
7. Bureaux de bienfaisance.
8. Etablissements hospitaliers.
9. Médicine gratuite.
10. Etablissements nationaux de bienfaisance.
11. Aliénés.
12. Dépôts de Mendicité.
13. Monts-de-piété
14. Etablissemenls libres.
15. Syndicat de communes.
16. Séance d'ouverture de conseil.
17 and 18. Enfants maltraités ou moralement abandonnés.
19. Dépôts de mendicité.
20. Mont-de-piété de Paris.
21. Extension des attributions des Inspecteurs des Enfants Assistés.
22. Assistance medicale dans les campagnes.
23. Révision de la Législation des Enfants assistés.
24. Statistique des dépenses publiques d'assistance en 1885.
25. Questions traitées dane la première session de 1889 par le Conseil.
26. Réunion administrative des bureaux de bienfaisance et des hôpitaux.
27 and 28. Enfants assistés.
29. Médicine gratuite.
30. Aliénés.
31. Questions traités dans la dernière session par le Conseil.

Interior, struck this note in an address to the council on June 13, 1888[386].

"In opening your first session let me remind you that you are descended from the French Revolution, and that you should work with perseverance to realize at last its conceptions, to execute the testament it has bequeathed ......The works of this grand . . . . commission[387], which represent on this question the views of the French Revolution, ... still astonish us by the elevation of their ideas, and, one may say, by the perfection of their means. . . . . . Unfortunately the cruel necessities of the national defense put an end to these wide plans. Later the military ente prises of the empire and the narrow preoccupations of rival dynasties too often turned aside the attention of legislators and politicians. When the spirit of the revolution reappeared for a moment in 1848, a fresh attempt was made to give a new impulse to the great principle of social solidarity, and to establish a general organization of what were then known as *seconrs publics*. Since then no law . . . . . containing a complete system of public assistance has been passed. It is bit by bit that the present law bus come into being, and yet it is truly the spirit of the revolution which lives in these fragments. In each of the branches of public assistance it is the memory of the principles laid down by the Constituent Assembly which regulates the relation between benefactor and beneficiary.

"But in the whole what gaps, what imperfections on every hand! The care of the insane is departmental but not obligatory, the care of assisted children is also departmental and also is not obligatory. If the departments give it an inadequate organization they cannot be made to do any better. . . . . It is time to coordinate all generous efforts, it is imperative to no longer leave to a chance benevolence the accomplishment of a social duty."

But the council has not confined itself to these more general utterances, but has put on record its '

approval of certain specific plans. It desires to see established a corps of departmental inspectors with power to supervise, "under the authority of the prefect and the control of the general inspectors," all the institutions coming within the scope of the direction of public assistance, and with the right to enter "avec voix consultative" all the

---

[386]Sixteenth *fascicule* of the Conseil Supérieur d'Assistance Publique.
[387]That is, the *Comité pour l'extinction de la Mendicité*, with La Rochefoucauld-Liancourt at its head, appointed by the National Assembly.

"commissions hospitalières" of each department[388].

The council has also agreed on the necessity of making medical assistance obligatory in the country districts and on the following points in regard to it[389]. The commune, in default of the family, owes assistance to the sick poor having settlement within its borders; the conseil général of the department should annually determine the respective shares of department and communes in the expenses, these expenses to be obligatory on the communes and imposable *d'office*; the government should have the right to impose a system if the department failed to organize one for itself within a certain length of time[390].

In its nineteenth "fascicule" the council reports resolutions to the effect that beggary be forbidden "on the territory of the republic," that a "bureau d' assistance" should be established in each commune or union of communes, and that workhouses (maisons de travail) should be instituted[391].

These propositions and the speeches quoted above clearly demonstrate the tendency of the present authorities toward a systematized and obligatory scheme of public assistance. All progress in this direction is, however, sure to meet with active and determined opposition from all those who believe, on general grounds, in a strict limitation of governmental functions, and this is the general position of French

---

[388]'Fascicule 25 quoted by Lallemand, *Réforme Sociale*, January 16, 1891, p. 142.

M. Monod, Director of Public Assistance, speaking before the internation *Congrès de Bienfaisance*, said that "in regard to public aid the excessive authority of the departments, communes and public institutions is at the expense of the unfortunate." Proceedings, Vol. 1, p. 280.

[389] A bill to institute a system of obligatory medical charity was brought before the Chamber of Deputies in June, 1890. In its *exposé de motifs* it was carefully explained that "the affirmation of social duty" does not imply recognition of a right to assistance on the part of the person aided. The bill, however, provides that any taxpayer can have an inquiry made into the case of any person omitted from the list of those who, having a settlement, "*doicent être secourus*" in case of sickness. See Lallemand, *Réforme Sociale*, January 16, 1891, p. 148.

See also Hubert-Valleroux, "La Charité avant et depuis 1789, dans les campagnes de France," p. 315. The international *Congrès de Bienfaisance* of 1889, voted that "L'assistance publique doit être rendue obligatoire par la loi pour les indigents temporairement ou définitivement incapables physiquement de pourvoir aux nécessités de l'existence." Proceedings, I, p. 559.

[390]Lallemand, *Réforme Sociale*, January 16, 1891, p. 143.

[391]Hubert-Valleroux, "La Charité avant et depuis 1789, dans les campagnes de France," p. 315.

publicists, upon whom the idea of a socialized state has as yet made very little impression compared with its progress in Germany, England, or even the United States. The Catholics, too, and all who resent the aggressive anti-religious measures of the past years, are earnest in their opposition to any further advance of governmental agencies into what they consider the proper field of the church and of private initiative.

Discontent is also felt at the attitude taken toward private charity and at the tendency of some officials, at least, to look upon relief-giving as a state monopoly to be jealously guarded from infringement.

The "Representation of the Poor,"1 and the Relation of Public and Private Charity.

The maire of the commune, who is president of the bureau de bienfaisance where one exists, is the legally constituted representative of the poor of the commune[392], and to him belongs the charge of any donations or legacies bestowed upon the poor without further specification, or, in their behoof, upon an institution or society not authorized to hold property or whose prerogatives do not include relief-giving. The legal points involved in this seemingly simple statement are many and difficult and have been hotly debated and, at different periods, differently resolved. The actual application of the principle may be best illustrated by concrete cases cited by Eavarin as representing the meaning of the law[393].

One case was that of a M. Hubert, a notary of Paris, who left a legacy of 200,000 francs for the benefit of poor working men, these

---

[392]In the early part of 1891, when the suffering from the unusual cold and consequent want of employment was at its height, the walls of Paris were covered with appeals from the maires of the different arrondissements for money or other help for the poor. There had already been a general placarding, in November, I think, announcing the official house-to-house collection in their behalf, and bespeaking a generous reception for the collectors, but the exceptional needs of the season made necessary a second call upon the public.

[393]Cf. Ravarin, "L'Assistance Communale en France," Chap. VII. "De la Representation des Pauvres," pp. 241-L'6.

to be chosen by his universal legatee "to the exclusion of the bureau de bienfaisance and of all administrative authorities whatever." The excluding clause was annulled as illegal, and the maire, as the only person competent to accept the legacy in behalf of the poor, took charge of the bequest.

In another case money was left to the well known order of the Little Sisters of the Poor, which, though properly incorporated, was not legally established in the parish in question. The will being interpreted as intending the legacy for the poor, not for the sisters in their own persons, the maire stepped in. In such cases the maire, though the legal recipient of the money, is supposed to see that it is expended as nearly as possible in conformity with the wishes of the testator. But the animosities too often existing between the civil and religious authorities would suggest, even without the presence of such stipulations as that of the will first referred to, that the fact of the intervention of the maire might materially affect the application of the funds.

The third case, that of a society authorized to receive bequests but not incorporated for objects of charity, is most important, as it involves the rights of the churches, both Protestant and Catholic. The French law in regard to "moral persons" or corporations is very strict, for they are the object of a traditional mistrust, and an authorization to receive legacies and hold property gives the right to do so only for the specified ends of the corporation. The question whether charity is one of the proper ends for which the church is constituted has been in dispute ever since the Concordat, and has been finally decided in the negative, so that money left to a Calvinist presbytery or Catholic *fabrique* (vestry) for the benefit of the poor could not legally be accepted by either.

Moreover it has been claimed that the bureau de bienf aisance—or where none exists the maire—alone has a right to have collections taken up or subscriptions solicited for the poor[394]. The church au-

---

[394] Cf. an article in the *Revue général le l'administration* (t. Ill, 1888), quoted by M. Hubert Valleroux (*loc. cit.* p. 271): "Les administrateurs ont le droit

thorities have no right even to refuse a request on the part of a bureau de bienfaisance for a church collection for its benefit[395].

Outside the disabilites above mentioned non-governmental charity is not forbidden, but it is strictly at the mercy of the authorities. Any charitable institution not duly authorized, even though carried on by an individual, is in an "irregular situation," and liable to be suppressed, since it might be so instituted as to "cross and interfere with the views of the government, and its principles in this important part of the administration[396]."

But it is chiefly by means of societies that charitable plans of any importance can be attempted, and the law in regard to societies is extremely arbitrary. By article 291 of the Penal Code no society of more than twenty persons, meeting periodically to occupy itself with any object, religious, literary, political or other, can be formed except with the consent of government and under such conditions as it may please the public authority to impose. The authorization confers no privileges but the bare right to meet as a society, and may be at any time withdrawn. It is moreover (or so it is said) often difficult to obtain, as the authorities prefer to assume no responsibility. To be able to hold property a society must receive "recognition as of public utility[397]," by a decree of the council of state, a recognition usually granted only after a society has proved itself by an existence of some years and on condition that a full account of the constitution and aims

---

de compter sur l'aide de la puissance publique et sur sa protection contre la *concurrence illegale* du clergé. L'Eglise a intérêt à faire des quêtes de charité pour affirmer son indépendance vis-a-vis de la loi laïque, pour établir sa préten-due vocation au rôle de bienfaitrice. . . . Il importe que les pouvoirs publics répriment tous les empiètements du clergésur les attributions des bureaux de bienfaisance et maintiennent à ces établissements le droit exclusif de faire dans les églises les quêtes de charité car il s' agit ici de l'intérêt sacré des pauvres."

Ravarin, however, cites a decision of the Council of State in 18S0, as denying to the bureau "le monopole de la charité, c'est-à-dire le droit de concentrerdans ses caisses les sommes recueillies publiquement par les particuliersau profit des pauvres," and as implying "*en faveur du curé, comme de tout citoyen, le droit de queterpour les indigents.*"

Cf. "L'Assistance Communale en France,"p. 230.

[395] See Block, "Dictionnaire de l'Administration Française," article "Quêtes."

[396] Fascicule 4 of the Conseil Supérieur d'Assistance Publique, quoted by Hubert-Valleroux, *loc. cit.*, p. 275.

[397] Cf. Block, "Dictionnaire de l'Administration Française," articles "Personne Civile," and "Etablissements Publics et d'Utilitè Publique."

of the society be submitted to the criticism of the authorities, who have the right to prescribe any changes in its internal arrangements that they choose, either then or at any later time. After having been "recognized" the society is not only liable to suppression and confiscation at their discretion, it has not even then the right to receive any gift or legacy without a special authorization[398]. "This rule," says Block ("Dictionnaire de l'Administration Française," article "Dons et Legs") "is justified by the interest of families, whose spoliation must be prevented, and by social and economic interests which are opposed to the excessive development of mainmorte, and to an increase of wealth beyond the needs or the mission of the institutions."

In addition to these disadvantages private charity. at least as embodied in societies or institutions, has to bear an extraordinary accumulation of taxes[399]. First there is no exemption from the regular taxes on donations and bequests, on contracts, on real estate, or from municipal taxes, etc. Beside these there is a special tax on "biens de mainmorte" amounting to 87½ per cent. of the real estate tax[400]. Moreover there is a tax of 3 per cent. on the profits made by societies of all sorts, railway companies for instance. By a law of 1884 charitable societies are made subject to this law, the collectors being instructed to estimate their profits as equal to 5 per cent. *at least* of the gross value of their buildings and furnishings[401].

Yet in spite of the difficulties thrown in its way private charity is,

---

[398] This is equally true of public institutions. What this means in practice is illustrated by a case cited as typical by Hubert-Valleroux, "La Charité avant et depuis 1789 dans les campagnes de France," p. 280. A man died leaving no heirs at law but only some cousins to whom he left sums varying from 20,000 to 100,000 francs, expressly excepting one cousin however, alleging that he had shown constant ingratitude toward the testator, and that he had, moreover, a fortune sufficient to satisfy not only his needs but his whims. The great part of the fortune was left to public charity. The council of state, however, allowed the public assistance of Paris to accept only three quarters of the bequest, and gave the rest, some 400,000 francs, to the cousins, including the one excluded by the will.

[399] The tax on entertainments given to raise money for charitable objects has been already spoken of. Cf. p. 81, note 1.

[400] Cf. Block, "Dictionnaire de l'Administration Française," article "Mainmorte (Taxe ou impôt des biens de)."

[401] Cf. Hubert-Valleroux, "La Charité avant et depuis 1789 dans les campagnes de France," p. 285 sq.

as has been seen, the patron and ally of public assistance. Not only are most of the funds of the latter drawn from private generosity, not only do public appropriations help support private charitable undertakings, but the whole system, if system it can be called, of public assistance implies and requires the existence of a private charity to which it is largely subsidiary[402].

Conclusion.

The foregoing pages have given some account of the form of public assistance in France. but to fill this out, to study its action and appreciate its effects would require wide personal experience of its workings, and fuller and more exact statistics than can be had.

Nevertheless some suggestions may be hazarded. A system of public relief must meet two tests; first, as to how far it relieves existing suffering, and secondly, as to whether it increases or diminishes the volume of preventable suffering, whether it pauperizes or educates. Even if these questions could be answered in regard to the French system, it would still be impossible to make international comparisons, unless the other elements of the differing situations of France and another country could be at least fairly analyzed.

Such answer as can be made on the first point is not very satisfactory. There is *no guarantee* in France against extreme and helpless suffering, except for certain classes of children and insane. More than a third of the population of France are without even a chance of public out-relief[403], and a far larger part without opportunity of refuge in a hospital or asylum[404]. Even where all the organs of public existence are in operation the relief afforded is commonly meagre and arbitrary, proportioned in its total amount not to the needs of the population as most wisely understood, but to the endowments that happen to be

---

[402]Cf. M. Bucquet's remarks, quoted p. 109.

[403]Cf. p. 100, note 1.

[404]Cf. p. 93 sq.

available. Thus a well-to-do village may have a bureau with a considerable income at its disposal for distribution, while another with many poor may have no bureau at all. The asylums are at least arbitrarily placed, and their capacity has no equally necessary relation to the numbers who need their shelter, so that those who are not admitted are often as worthy and as needy as others who are received, and who owe their advantage merely to an accidental priority.

On the second and more important count it is still harder to pass judgment. The general impression would be, I suppose, that France had not suffered to anything like the same extent as England from the curse of pauperization. Such an impression is singularly hard to verify, and if it could be verified would not necessarily prove either system superior, so largely do economic and racial peculiarities enter into the question. In both France and England the proportion of paupers to the population seems to have been falling. The figures of the bureaux de bienfaisance of Paris are fairly reliable, though something must be allowed for different policies as to permitting enrollment on the list of *indigents*, and these show a very fair improvement. As given by Levasseur[405] they are as follows for this century—

Proportion of *indigents* to the population of the city:

1804......	15.8 per cent.	1861......	5.3 per cent.
1813......	16.5 "	1869......	6.1 "
1818......	12.1 "	1872......	5.4 "
1829......	7.9 "	1880......	5.5 "
1835......	6.9 "	1886......	5.9 "
1847......	7.9 "	1887......	4.1 "
1850......	6.1 "		

It will be noticed that the exceptions to the declining proportion generally mark years preceding political crises, 1813, 1847, 1869.

It' would seem that at least the assistance of the bureau de bienfaisance, with the service of unpaid visitors and the absence of all legal character, must be better than relief from rates, unless the latter was exceptionally well administered, but even this seems to be

---

[405]See Levasseur, "La Population Française," t. III, p. 138.

doubtful. De Watteville, in his great report of 1847[406], speaks of the doles of the bureaus as follows: "As for the general annual average of 10.42 francs, 2.28 francs being subtracted for general administrative expenses, it is entirely insufficient, and one may say boldly that if the average in question were not distributed to the poor they would not be the worse off for this. So that what is called 'assistance à domicile' is commonly considered ineffectual. It may be affirmed that the pauper would not suffer any more if this inconsiderable aid, distributed so uniformly and with a complete lack of intelligence, ceased to be given monthly. In the sixty years that the administration of out-relief has been carried on there has never been seen a single pauper taken out of his want and supporting himself through the efforts and aid of this sort of charity. On the contrary this often *constitutes hereditary pauperism.* So we find to-day on the registers of this administration the grandsons of paupers admitted to public relief in 1802, while the sons had been, in 1830, similarly set down on these fatal tables."

We have seen that Bucquet[407], in his report of 1870, while not accusing relief of inducing pauperism, yet also admits that it does little to end it. Testimony of another and very valuable sort is that of Edward Denison, an expert in English poor law, who visited France in 1868 especially to study French public assistance. He came prepared to admire and returned feeling himself completely disillusioned and rating the French method "even beneath our own." After a second visit he wrote to a friend, "I have burst the bubble I went to see in France. It is a shambling approach to workhouse and poor-rate under color of voluntary effort. We have hardly anything to learn from France, *except the natural thrift of the people, which makes the collective insurance of poor-rate unnecessary*[408]." It might be asked whether the the absence of such insurance through generations were not part cause of this national thriftiness and good management, but

---

[406] "Rapport à son Ex. le Ministre de l'Intérieur sur l'Administration des Bureaux de Bienfaisance et sur la Situation du Paupérisme en France, par le Baron de Watteville, inspecteur général des établissements de bienfaisance." Paris, Imprimerie Royale, 1854, p. 18.

[407] Cf. p. 109.

[408] "Letters and other writings of the late Edward Denison," p. 167.

probably these are rather a trait of the French character than a result of modern conditions.

Whatever may be the fact in regard to the quantity of pauperism in France, it certainly seems less lamentable in quality than that of England, but this is undoubtedly partly due to a gift related to thriftiness, the power of keeping up appearances and pride in doing so.

In this regard the elasticity in the administration of aid made possible by its voluntary character may conceivably be advantageous. On the other hand the existence of endowments, making possible the inscription of a whole village on the pauper roll, is a misfortune that could not happen under a system of poor-rates.

It is easy enough to point out the incompleteness and inconsistencies of the French system, and they have been constantly commented on by French writers, both by critics and students, and by the authorities, who wish to make sweeping charges. One of the most vulnerable points has been strengthened by the law of 1890 on the *syndicats de communes*, which makes it possible for small communities to cooperate in the care of their poor. Charges of extravagance, dishonesty and political and religious bias in the administration of relief are not lacking. The fact that private charity is mainly religious, and that the government has been for the last twenty years bitterly anti-religious, has naturally had a very unfortunate effect, preventing cooperation and giving a partisan edge to criticism which makes it the more difficult to judge the situation.

There is undoubtedly room for many particular reforms, many of which have been discussed already, but whether, under existing circumstances, an attempt to make a complete and consistent system would not be a grave misfortune may well be doubted. The French could hardly bring to the task of reconstruction that experience of relief giving and its effects which exists in England, already digested and compared, in the minds and records of experts in poor law administration and organized charity; and the French love of symmetrical and logical schemes would be much to be dreaded, in case of such an attempt, especially in view of the radical, not to say communistic.

132

strain in the inheritance of the republic.

I have said that the French do not possess the store of experience on a special point gathered in England. This is partly because their attention has been largely concentrated on different sides of the problem from those that have most interested English and American thinkers.

It is because the problems of social pathology, which are common to all nations arrived at somewhat the same stage in their evolution, are studied with different preoccupations and under a different light in France, as well as because French solutions have their practical lessons for us, that the public charity of France is so worthy of more thorough study than has been possible in this monograph.

www.ingramcontent.com/pod-product-compliance
Lightning Source LLC
Chambersburg PA
CBHW050233270326
41914CB00033BB/1894/J